The
BOBBY JONES
ON GOLF

FOREWORD BY JACK NICKLAUS
and an Introduction by Robert T. Jones IV
Edited by Sidney L. Matthew

CITADEL PRESS
Kensington Publishing Corp.
www.kensingtonbooks.com

ACKNOWLEDGMENTS

Grateful appreciation is extended to Robert Tyre Jones IV, who graciously contributed the Introduction; Grand Ad Graphics of Tallahassee, who contributed to the prepress; Gwynne Chason and Cindy Thompson for assistance in manuscript preparation; Edward Kasper, whose genius produced the artwork; Jonesheirs, Inc. for their cooperation in these endeavors; TO GOD BE THE GLORY.

The Foreword is reprinted with permission of Jack Nicklaus and Herbert Warren Wind and is from *The Greatest Game of All: My Life in Golf*, Simon and Schuster, New York, 1969, whose permission is gratefully acknowledged by the Editor.

Also gratefully acknowledged is material excerpted from *Bobby Jones on Golf* by Bobby Jones, copyrighted 1966 by Robert Tyre Jones, Jr., and used with permission of Doubleday, a Division of Bantam Doubleday Dell Publishing Group Inc.

Thanks to Sybervision (makers of those wonderful Bobby Jones instructional films) for permission to use the trademark "The Best of Bobby Jones."

Lastly, the Editor would like to dedicate this work to Charlie Yates, a wise–cracking, happy–go–lucky protégé of Bobby Jones down in Atlanta whose high spirits were so infectious that he accomplished the unprecedented feat of standing on the steps of the Royal and Ancient Clubhouse at St. Andrews after the 1938 Walker Cup match and inducing the crowd to accompany him in *A Wee Doch and Doris*... "Lang may yer lum reek"

TABLE OF CONTENTS

FOREWORD

[From *The Greatest Game of All: My Life in Golf*, Simon and
Schuster, New York, 1969. Reprinted with permission of
Jack Nicklaus and Herbert Warren Wind]

My first golf hero was Bob Jones, and this, of course, was a
very fortunate thing. I became aware of Jones in 1950
when I started golf at the age of ten, for my father was a member of the Scioto Country Club in Columbus, Ohio, our
hometown, and it was there that Jones had won the 1926
United States Open. It was a wonderful victory in many ways.
First, Bobby—he was in his mid-twenties then, and he was
known to everyone as Bobby—made a fine driving finish over
the last nine holes to pick up five shots on the leader, Joe Turnesa, and edge him out by one. On top of this, earlier that
season Jones had won the British Open at Lytham & St.
Anne's, and with his victory at Scioto he made golf history by
becoming the first man to carry off the two big national
championships in the same year.

In any event, Scioto never forgot Bobby Jones. When I became a member of the club, a full twenty-four years had
elapsed since Jones' victory, but a photograph of him still
hung in a prominent position in the locker room, and another in the pro shop. The latter showed him at the finish of
his follow-through on a drive. (I think it must be the photo
General Eisenhower used as a model for his famous painting
of Jones that is on display in Golf House, the United States
Golf Association's headquarters in New York City.) In addition
to this, many of the older members of Scioto, who had been
deeply impressed by both Jones' golf and his personal charm,
were always talking about him. The most devoted of these
Jones-men was Stanley Crooks, a very capable golfer, by the

way, who won the club championship several times. He was a good friend of Jones' and corresponded with him, and, if anything, the passing years had sharpened his memory of Bobby's performance back in 1926. He knew every one of the 293 shots Jones had hit.

When I first showed some promise in golf, Mr. Crooks began to tell me more and more about Jones—where he liked to place his drive on this hole and how he tried to play that hole; how he had missed his par on each of the four rounds on the relatively easy 145-yard ninth; how Bobby thought one of the best holes on the course was the eighth, a long par 5, where a virtual wheat field bordered the right side of the fairway off the tee and where, in second shot range, a stream crossed the fairway and then curled to the left around the back of the green; and above all, how Bobby, needing a birdie to win on the last hole, a 480-yard par 5 that Turnesa had birdied just previously, laced out a drive that was fully 300 yards long, followed it with a 4-iron 15 feet past the pin, and got down in two safe putts. In 1950, I should bring out, Scioto had changed very little from the course Jones had tackled, and knowing how he had played it was a spur to me. It is a definite advantage for a young golfer, I believe, to grow up on a championship course, and there is something of additional value to be gained from knowing how a champion played the different holes. It gives you something concrete to measure your progress against.

Along with Stanley Crooks, there were two men at Scioto who never stopped talking about Jones. One was Jack Grout, a tall, scholarly-looking Oklahoman who became the pro at Scioto the same year I took up the game. Jack was a tireless student of the golf swing. While he kept very much abreast of the times and was fascinated by the mechanics of Nelson's swing and Snead's and Hogan's, there were several respects in which he felt Jones' technique had never been improved on, and he made this very clear to his pupils. The other notorious Jones enthusiast was my father. The year the Open was held at

Scioto, he was a boy of thirteen. He had played a little golf on
the public courses, and for him, as for so many other Ameri-
cans, there was no one like Bobby Jones. Through the kind-
ness of the pharmacist he worked for after school hours, Dad
got tickets for the Open, and he stayed on Jones' heels all
four rounds. Watching his hero in action was the greatest experience of his young life, and it remained evergreen in his
mind. I imagine his identification with Jones became all the
stronger because of an offbeat incident that took place at
Scioto when the Ryder Cup Match was played there in 1931.
Jones, who had come up from Atlanta for the event, was
twenty-nine at the time. There couldn't have been too much
resemblance, really, between him and my dad, then just eighteen. However, my dad had the same chunky build as Jones,
he parted his hair down the middle like Jones, and on this
particular day he happened to be wearing knickers like
Jones—and darned if the attendant at the front door of the
clubhouse didn't sing out,"Yessir, Mister Jones," when my dad
approached and fling the door open for him with a flourish.
Dad's ticket didn't include clubhouse privileges, and he had
just been edging up to take a squint inside. With the entrance
suddenly opened, he tossed the attendant a friendly smile, the
way he thought Jones would have, and sauntered around the
clubhouse for an hour, taking it all in.

For all these reasons, when I started playing golf I knew
more about Robert T. Jones, Jr., than I did about any of the
current champions. Later that year I learned a good deal
about Ben Hogan, of course. This was the season, 1950, that
Ben returned to golf after his near-fatal accident sixteen
months earlier and then proceeded to astound the sports
world by winning the U.S. Open at Merion. I also knew a little
about Jimmy Demaret—very little; I knew he wore bright
clothes and might stride onto the first tee any day wearing
one blue shoe and one green shoe. Beyond this, the other
"name golfers" were just a blur to me. That summer, however,
I got a firsthand look at many of them, for Scioto was host to

another championship, the 1950 P.G.A. (That was the year Chandler Harper beat Henry Williams, Jr., in the final.) By this time my dad was a member of the club, so there was no problem about the front door, but the locker room was off limits except for the players. However, Skip Alexander, one of the top touring pros, saw me with my autograph book at the door and put his arm around my shoulder and led me into the locker room. With Skip's help, I got the autographs of nearly all the players. Outside of how pleasant and considerate Skip was, little else sticks in my mind. I remember watching Lloyd Mangrum playing cards, a tall drink in one hand and cigarette dangling from his lips beneath his moustache. It was a picture that would make an impression on any ten-year-old boy—there he was, the complete riverboat gambler come to life. I also remember catching a glimpse of Sam Snead. Sam couldn't have had too good a day. He was scowling and silent, and he was in and out of the locker room in thirty seconds.

Soon after that P.G.A. Championship, my friend Skip Alexander almost lost his life in an airplane crash. Although he made a phenomenal recovery from his injuries, he never regained full use of his hands and fingers, and his career as a tournament golfer was over. Skip stayed in the game, though. Today he is the pro at the Lakewood Country Club in St. Petersburg, Florida, and I get to see him when he comes over to the Palm Beach area for a tournament or a pro-am. Skip usually stays with my neighbor at Lost Tree Village, Cary Middlecoff.

I did not meet Bob Jones until five years later, in 1955, when I qualified for the United States Amateur Championship for the first time. It took place that year at the James River course of the Country Club of Virginia, in Richmond. Since 1955 marked the twenty-fifth anniversary of Jones' last appearance in that championship—his victory in the 1930 Amateur, at Merion, was the fourth and final trick in his incredible Grand Slam—the U.S.G.A. had asked him to come

up from Atlanta and speak at the Players' Dinner. He undoubtedly would have honored this request anyway, but I have
a feeling that the fact that this was one of the rare occasions
when a national championship was being held in the South
contributed to Jones' decision to attend. The day before the
start of the tournament, when the field was getting in its final
warm-up rounds, Jones parked his golf cart behind the last
green to take in some of the play on that hole, a 460-yard par
4 over breaking, hilly ground. It so happened that I hit the
eighteenth green that afternoon with two good woods and,
furthermore, that during the time that Jones was watching, no
other player had got home in two. He asked a newspaperman
with him who I was, and on learning that I was only fifteen
years old, he said he would like to talk with me. My father and
I went over together. This session with Jones was a tremendous thrill for me, but I am sure it meant twice as much to my
dad. Our chat lasted about twenty minutes—a good deal of it
was about Scioto, naturally—and then Jones turned to me and
said, "Young man, I've heard that you're a fine golfer. I'm
coming out and watch you play a few holes tomorrow."

My first-round opponent was Bob Gardner, a Californian
who had moved to the New York area, a well-grounded golfer
who was subsequently a teammate of mine in the 1960 Eisenhower Trophy and the 1961 Walker Cup matches. We had
quite a battle that day in Richmond. At the end of the first
nine we were even, and then I went 1 up by birdieing the
tenth. As we walked to the eleventh, there was Bob Jones sit-
ting in his golf cart on the edge of the tee. I wanted to play my
very best in front of him, and I thought I might, for I'd been
hitting the ball straight and crisp that morning.

Well, it didn't work out quite that way. I missed my par on
the eleventh, a 412-yard par 4, when I took three from just off
the green. I lost that hole to Gardner's par. On the twelfth, a
par 4, 423 yards long, uphill most of the way, I was even more
brilliant—I took a double bogey: a drive pushed into the trees
on the right, a choppy recovery, an underclubbed approach,

and three more to get down from the apron. I lost that hole, too. The thirteenth is a short par 4 that doglegs sharply to the right as it falls down a hillside to a ticklish little green. I was weak with my second, and when I stubbed my chip, I had lost three holes in a row and gone from 1 up to 2 down. Jones left at this point. As he later told my father, he felt that his presence might have led me to try too hard. After treating him to that splendid run of bogey, double bogey, bogey, I managed to settle down, and won two of the next four holes to square the match. Then I lost it on the eighteenth when I hit my tee-shot into heavy rough and couldn't get home with my second. Gardner played it perfectly, an excellent drive and an excellent fairway wood onto the green, and that was that.

My next meeting with Bob Jones took place some two years later when he spoke at the banquet held in connection with the 1957 International Jaycees Junior Championship, which was played on the Ohio State University course. (We had our picture taken together, and it hangs today in my game room.) Then, another two years later, I qualified for the Masters for the first time, so I was able to get together with Jones that spring—and in the springs that followed until 1962—at the Amateurs' Dinner on the Wednesday night before the start of the Masters. Sometimes we just talked. I remember, for example, his reminiscing about the 1926 Open one evening and recalling that the wheat field of rough on the eighth hole was so high that on one round, after his caddie had laid down his bag in the rough so that they could better help Bob's playing partner find his ball, they had an awful time finding the bag. Other times we talked a bit more seriously. However, the most helpful piece of advice I received from Bob came to me secondhand, through my father. "I think I was a fairly good young golfer," Jones told him one evening, "but I never became what I would call a really good golfer until I had been competing for quite a number of seasons. You see, when I first started to play in the big tournaments, whenever anything went wrong, I'd run home to

Stewart Maiden, our pro at East Lake. Finally, I matured to the point where I understood my game well enough to make my own corrections during the course of a tournament, and *that's* when I'd say I became a *good* golfer."

When my dad relayed this conversation to me, it made a particularly strong impression because whenever something had gone wrong in a tournament, I had run home to Jack Grout. From the time Jack started to give me lessons, he wanted me to understand the mechanics of the swing, and, for my part, I wanted to learn all about them—why you made this movement in the swing, or what effect that movement produced. I wanted to be able to take care of myself out on the course. Somehow, though, I was still always running back to Jack Grout to fix me up. This is why Jones' statement hit me so right. It made me much more determined to learn everything I could about my swing so that, to some extent, I could diagnose my own errors and put myself back on my game. I cannot tell you what a big factor this is in tournament play. It may be the biggest factor of all in shaping success or failure in the crucible of competition.

Bob Jones—I never call him anything but Mr. Jones—possesses the gift of intimacy and is always doing little things that make you feel that you are an old friend with whom he can be humorous, or frank, or spontaneous, as the case may be. One small illustration that comes to mind involved Bob only indirectly. In the 1959 Amateur, at Broadmoor, through the accident of the draw I came up against his son, Robert T. Jones, III, in the first round. Young Bob is a very good player who has qualified for the Amateur quite a few times, and on his day he can give any golfer all that he can handle. That morning at Broadmoor when young Bob and I met on the first tee, he greeted me with a big, warm smile. "You might be interested in knowing, Jack," he said, "that my father was thinking of coming out for this tournament. Then when he found out who I had drawn as my first opponent, he changed his mind.

He decided it wasn't worth a trip to Colorado just to watch me play one round."

More to the point was a letter I received from Bob Jones shortly after I had broken through in the 1962 U.S. Open. If my victory hinged on any one single stroke, it was the four-foot putt I had to hole on the 71st green to save my par, stay even with Arnold Palmer, and set up a playoff. It was an extremely tough putt: it broke a little left and then, near the hole, it broke back to the right off a little rise. The more I studied the putt, the more convinced I became that, especially under the pressure, I probably wouldn't be able to handle that double roll with the exceptional delicacy it required. My best chance would be to rap the ball so firmly that neither the left or right break could really take effect. I hit the ball hard, for the back of the cup, and it fell—and if it hadn't, it would have gone miles past, it was moving that fast. As I say, I thought this was the pivotal stroke of the tournament for me, so it pleased me enormously when Bob Jones gave it primary emphasis in a letter of congratulation he sent me shortly afterward. Watching on TV, he had recognized exactly what my problem was and the risk I took in trying to solve it the way I did. "When I saw the ball dive into the hole," he wrote, "I almost jumped right out of my chair." I can't recall a letter that made me feel as good as that one did.

Apart from whatever other talks we may have at the Masters each year, I generally get to see Bob out on the course. When you come to the most dangerous stretch, the passage from the eleventh through the thirteenth, Bob is usually out there in his golf cart, studying you closely. Quite often, he'll pick you up on the fifteenth and sixteenth, too. I have managed to play some acceptable golf in front of him, but I know he was also watching when I hit one of the rottenest shots of my life—an 8-iron on the short twelfth in the 1964 Masters that I shanked so beautifully I still had a pretty full pitch left over Rae's Creek to the green. (I got my 4, one of the best bogeys I've ever made.) Because of my admiration for Bob

Jones, the Masters—the tournament he created, played on the course he helped design—has always been something unbelievably special for me. When I have been fortunate enough to win it, I have treasured not only the victory itself but the generous things he has said about my play at the presentation ceremony. When Bob says something about your golf, you know there is substance and sincerity in it.

Above and beyond this, you always feel that he understands what you are all about as a man, as well as a golfer. This gives everything a deeper meaning, and it sticks to your bones.

Looking back on my friendship with Bob Jones, I am increasingly aware what a lucky thing it was for me that he happened to win one of his Opens at Scioto so that from the beginning, despite the differences in our ages, there was always a bond between us. I have learned an awful lot from him. We all have. More than any other person in our time, he has served to give us a sense of continuity with the game's earlier eras and its earlier players, to make us feel a part of an immensely worthwhile tradition. In a word, he has embodied the spirit of golf.

—Jack Nicklaus

INTRODUCTION

I was pleased and honored when Sidney Matthew asked me to write the foreword to this volume, a collection of my grandfather's newspaper columns on the game of the golf. As thrilled as I was to have the opportunity to pen a few words, I was especially excited to see this project come to fruition. This marks the first time that these newspaper columns have been published since their original composition and the first time that they have been collected in this form.

Whenever I play golf at a new course and someone discovers who my grandfather was, I am invariably asked, "Just how good was Bobby Jones, really?" I was thirteen years old when I asked my father that same question. "Dad, how good was Bub (our family nickname for grandfather)?"

Dad told me of a conversation to which he was privy between Ben Hogan and Bub at the Champions' Dinner at a Master's Tournament. He said that Bub and Hogan were discussing how they had played several different golf holes, and they came to a discussion of the 17th on the Old Course at St. Andrews, the famed "Road Hole."

"I was listening to their discussion," my father said, "and they were debating how to play the approach shot to the green. Dad stated that he felt that the best way to play that shot is to keep the ball on the club face just a little bit longer than normal. Hogan was nodding his head in agreement, and the significance of what they were saying just floored me."

The tournament player and the good club player can intentionally make the ball do many amazing things, but I am hard-pressed to name a player other than Bub and Hogan with the "feel" to determine how long the ball is on the face of the club!

Now, what about Bub as a writer? In these pages you will read columns that he wrote during the 1920s. There is a freshness and a spontaneity to these columns that is refreshing. In these columns, the reader is introduced to the thinking of Bobby Jones when he was at the height of his athletic power. These columns demonstrate his remarkable ability to state complex ideas simply.

These articles will give the reader a better understanding of my grandfather's golf. I think it is important to remember that he was not a professional golfer or a golf instructor. The reader will also discover in these columns that my grandfather was a thoughtful student of all facets of the game. My grandfather pioneered the use of steel shafted clubs, and even associated his name to the project and helped with their design. Additionally, he was the first person to set his name on registered, swing-weight matched clubs. These allowed the golfer to have a set of clubs where one club would feel like another of the same set.

This year, 1996, marks the 25th anniversary of my grandfather's death. Yet these columns, I think, are living documents. It is my hope that these essays will give the reader a glimpse into the workings of my grandfather's mind, and maybe help shave a few strokes off the reader's handicap.

Finally, I wish to say a few words about the editor of this work, my dear friend Sidney Matthew. No one has worked more diligently to understand my grandfather, both as a man and as an athlete, than Sid Matthew. Sid is an accomplished trial lawyer, a gentleman, and a "gritty" golfer. His love for the game of golf and his love for my grandfather are evident in the quality of his work, and are only exceeded by his devotion to his family and his commitment to friendship. I am honored to claim Sidney as a friend and I thank him for his efforts in these projects.

—Robert Tyre Jones IV

LIST OF TERMS

brassie: a wooden club with a brass soleplate designed to protect the club from fracture when a stroke is played from a road or other hard surface; more lofted than the driver.

cuppie lie: a ball lying in a shallow hollow such as may have been made by some former player having cut out a piece of turf.

long iron: an iron club with little loft designed to drive the ball long distances with a low trajectory and much roll; it has the longest shaft of all iron clubs but not longer than a driver.

mashie: a moderately lofted iron club shorter in the blade than a mid-iron; it is approximately the loft of a modern number five iron.

more lofted club: a club whose face has more angulation and is designed to drive the ball on a higher trajectory, resulting in less roll when the ball strikes the green.

niblick: a club used for bunkers, hazards, and high lofted strokes; the head is small and round, with a great deal of loft; roughly equivalent to a modern number nine iron.

spade shot: a lofted stroke causing the ball to spin and stop without roll; the club has the loft of a modern seven iron.

spoon: a wooden club with a more lofted face than a straight faced driver; the spoon strikes between the ball and the ground, causing backspin on the ball, which stops on the green without roll.

stymie: the position of adversaries' golf balls wherein the opponent's ball lies directly in the intended line of play of the other player's ball in relation to the hole.

ON WHEN TO SEEK ADVICE FROM YOUR GOLF PROFESSIONAL

The general disrepute enjoyed by the kind of golfing advice that we designate as a "tip" has led a number of players to profess a distrust for all sorts of instruction. Real "tips" on golf do circulate almost as freely as "tips" on the stock market and horse races, and are equally worthless. But sound information is regarded as a "tip" by neither stock market operators nor golfers. Information concerning anything that interests us should always be welcome, be it pertaining to golf or to anything else.

> Naturally, the very best of instructors
> cannot construct or even overhaul an
> entire swing in one lesson.

A true "tip" was that offered by Stewart Maiden to a pupil with whom he had worn himself out without effecting any improvement. Having exhausted every conceivable means of coaching his pupil into something resembling a correct swing, and judging the task to be hopeless, at last he turned to him and asked (they knew each other quite well): "Do you absolutely have to play golf?" When the pupil replied that he did not know how he would survive if he had to give it up, Stewart told him to point the toe of his club at the ball and swing.

1

This was a "tip," not information about the correct swing—a last resort which might work for a while, but would do no lasting good. Of course Stewart knew this, and frankly offered it as such.

Pupil After Quick Remedy

But when an instructor tells a pupil to unwind his hips a bit more rapidly, or to cock his wrists as he swings the club back, or when he gives him any other bit of sound information, he is not offering a tip, and it should not be received as such. The average golfer only goes to his pro for quick corrections. He goes only when his game, instead of remaining bad, has become worse, and he wants something done about it in a half hour or less. Even in these circumstances a pro rarely resorts to tips. He tries to pick out the seat of the trouble, to find if possible the first cause and offer the advice which will correct it.

Naturally, the very best of instructors cannot construct or even overhaul an entire swing in one lesson. Given a pupil who already has a fair notion of how to hit a golf ball, and a swing which is badly off in only one place, the average pro in a relatively short time can effect a satisfactory improvement, but the moment he goes off again, he begins to suspect that the advice he received was entirely wrong. When he tries again and again what the pro has told him, and does so without success, he becomes convinced that it is all "bunk," and that he may as well work out his own salvation.

The Expert Gets Off

Not all professional instructors are miracle workers. This profession has its incompetents as well as any other. But what the average golfer should remember is that even the expert player who knows his own swing and who has the correct habits drilled into his muscles by dint of years of correct swinging, even a player like this gets off his game and sometimes stays off for quite a while.

> He goes only when his game, instead of remaining bad, has become worse, and he wants something done about it in a half hour or less.

The maddening thing about golf is that it cannot always be played successfully with the same conscious direction. By this I mean that at one time it will be necessary to concentrate directly upon the performance of this action, and at another time good results can be had only by focusing attention upon another action. One cannot possibly think through the entire swing each time a shot is played. The expert and experienced player soon finds out for himself the "conscious direction" which his swing requires. The average golfer, lacking a complete understanding of the swing, can apply only the direction which has been given him to overcome one particular faulty tendency. He cannot reasonably expect it to be everlastingly sufficient.

ON POSTING YOUR BEST SCORE

Why is it, someone asks, that so often after making an exceptionally good score on the first nine holes, a player apparently loses all touch with his game and comes home in astonishingly bad figures? Isn't it strange that this explosion should occur when he appears to be in his best stride? Apparently there is a lower limit fixed upon the score that a given person may turn in, and if he goes many strokes below his allotment in the early stages, it is more than likely that the closing will even the count.

> The man drawing up from the rear, on the other hand, finds himself in an aggressive frame of mind, with nothing to think about except playing golf.

Yet it is no such law of averages or anything like it which is responsible for the leveling process. It is almost impossible to measure the force with which the consciousness of a good score in the making weighs down upon the performer. The nearer he approaches his goal, the harder each shot becomes, until the meanest obstacles appear almost insurmountable. There is far less nervous strain involved in overcoming the ef-

4

fects of a bad start than in maintaining the standard set by a well-made beginning.

That mental pressure is responsible, more than anything else, for the fact that the third round leader rarely finishes in front of an open championship field. The thing that presses him down is not that he has "shot his bolt," as the saying goes, for if the fourth round were a separate affair with everyone starting even, he could probably do as well as anyone. But the thought of the few strokes lead which he must protect makes him overfearful and overcautious. The man drawing up from the rear, on the other hand, finds himself in an aggressive frame of mind, with nothing to think about except playing golf. Very often he can play himself into a winning position before he has time to appreciate the importance of what he is doing.

Forget Good and Bad Holes

The shopworn admonition to forget the last shot and play the one in hand was meant to apply as much to the good ones as to the bad. It is just as important to forget the threes as the sixes.

I have never forgotten the comment made to me several years ago by a very well-known professional. We had just heard at the clubhouse that Walter Hagen had run into a phenomenal string of sub-par holes. "You know, Bobby," said the pro, "the greatest thing about Hagen is that after he makes a few birdies he thinks he can keep on doing it, whereas if you or I do it, instead of continuing to play golf we begin to wonder if this isn't too good to be true. We begin to be suspicious of our good fortune and to expect a six or seven to jump up any minute."

Of course, one may say that it is easy to understand why there should be a considerable mental strain in a tournament, but the same conditions do not bear upon a Saturday afternoon of golf. It is a different situation, of course, but every golfer knows what it means to beat his best score over his home course. The putt which turns the trick is fully as momentous as was Johnny Farrell's on the last hole at Olympia Fields.

Overcome Mental Hazard

In 1916 my best score at East Lake was 74; not in competition, of course, and like anyone else, every time I went out to play I tried to beat it. I tried all that summer and all the next year without success. I remember at least four occasions when I stood on the seventeenth tee needing only two pars, a four and a three, not merely to beat 74 but to beat 70. Each time I arrived at that point I began to think of what I was about to do, and each time I would use up just enough strokes to bring my total up to 74. It was two full years before I could break through the barrier raised by that 74. If I could have refrained from thinking about it, I should have probably beat it in a few months.

So the average player's difficulty in breaking 90 or 85 is no different from the expert's trouble when he tries to win a championship. When I hear a man censured for collapsing in the last round of a competition when he apparently had it won, I always want to ask the critic if he has ever had three fives to beat his own best score, and if he got them. Whether the score is 70 or a 100 is of little moment. It's all a question of what it means.

On Proper Timing

It is unfortunate that the most important feature of the golf stroke is so difficult to explain or to understand. We all talk about good timing, and faulty timing, and the importance of timing, and yet no one has been able to fix upon a means of saying what timing is. The duffer is told that he spoils his shot because his stroke is not properly timed, but no one can tell him how he can time it properly.

One very common error which results in bad timing can, I believe, be pointed out with sufficient exactness at least to give the enterprising average golfer something to work on. I mean the error of beginning to hit too early in the downward stroke. I have said that it is a common error. It is an error common to all golfers, a chronic lapse in the case of the expert, but an unfailing habit in the case of the dub. I believe it will be found that of the players who turn in scores of ninety and over, ninety-nine out of every hundred hit too soon on ninety-nine out of every hundred strokes. Many who play even better golf and have really decent-looking form fail to play better than they do for this very reason.

Hitting Too Soon

Hitting too soon is a fault of timing in itself. It results in the player reaching the ball with a large part of the power of the stroke already spent. Instead of being able to apply it all behind the ball, he has expended a vast amount upon the air, where it could do no good. Apparently every one fears that he will not be able to strike out in time, when, as a matter of fact, there has not one single player come under my observation who has been habitually guilty of late hitting. Sometimes they fail to close the face of the club by the time the club reaches the ball, but this is always due to something entirely apart from tardy delivery.

The primary cause of this trouble is to be found in the action of the right hand and wrist. If the left hand has a firm grip upon the club, as long as it remains in control, there can be no premature hitting. The left side is striking backhanded and it will prefer to pull from the left shoulder with the left elbow straight, rather than to deliver a blow involving an uncocking of the wrist.

But the right hand throughout the stroke is in the more powerful position. Its part in the stroke is on what, in tennis, would be called the forehand. It is moving forward in the direction easiest for it to follow. Because the player is intent upon effort and upon hitting hard, the right hand tends to get into the fight long before it has any right to enter. The right hand must be restrained, if it is not to hit before its time arrives.

Increase Speed Gradually

I wish everyone could study carefully a few sets of motion pictures showing the proper action of the right side, noting particularly the successive positions of the wrists. In the case of an expert player, the wrists remain fully cocked, just as they were at the top of the swing, until at least half of the down-stroke has been completed by the arms.

The dub, on the other hand, starts immediately, when coming down, to whip the club with his wrists. He forthwith

8

takes all the coil out of his spring, and when his hands reach the position corresponding to the numeral eight on the dial of a watch, his wrists are perfectly straight, and all the power left is in his arms and shoulders, to be utilized by any twist or contortion the player can execute.

When once the sense is felt and the drives begin to crack sharply, the speed and force can be increased gradually up to the player's limit.

It is hard to wait as long as the player is expending anything like the maximum effort. It is therefore wise to work into this sense of delayed hitting by swinging, at first gently, toward the ball. I have seen numbers of mediocre players who were able to obtain fine results by exercising a bit of restraint. When once the sense is felt and the drives begin to crack sharply, the speed and force can be increased gradually up to the player's limit.

ON THE STRAIGHT LEFT ARM
AND SIDE IN THE STROKE

The motion picture camera shows beyond any doubt that a straight left at impact is an absolute necessity. We began to talk about the straight left long ago, but we were conscious of it then only because a few snapshots had shown the left arms of some experts to be straight at, or near the top of the swing, where the motion was slow enough to be properly photographed.

But little harm is done by a slight relaxation of the left at the top of the swing. Many first class players permit such a thing. But for controlled, accurate, and consistent hitting, the left arm simply must be straight when the clubhead meets the ball. And it seems to me to be sounder practice to maintain it so throughout the stroke, rather than to rely upon taking up even the least bit of slack during the downstroke.

> I think there can be no question that
> the golf stroke ought to be dominated
> from first to last by the left arm.

I am an extravagant admirer of the play of the youngest professional luminary, Horton Smith of Missouri, but it strikes me that Horton's left arm may be the cause of whatever troubles he has. Other people can score in the high seventies in competition without occasioning much comment, but young Smith's style is so simple, and his swing nearly always so well-ground, that one seeks a reason for his 78 in the second round at Hoylake and his 40 on the last nine of the third round at Interlachen. Each disaster put him practically out of the running at a time when his characteristic play had made him most formidable.

Early in the spring, George Sargent visited Atlanta and was led into a discussion of Smith's play. At that time I had seen him play very little, but Sargent had made a close study of his style. "Smith's left arm," said Sargent, "normally relaxes the smallest fraction of a second after he hits the ball. The margin in there is so close that I believe when the strain of competition falls upon him, his left arm may quit a bit too soon."

This conception of the straight left, hitting on past the position of the ball, is a more definite expression of the age-old idea of hitting through. It gives to the player an understanding of how he should hit through, and with what he should do it. To hit an inch through the ball is actually enough, but the more the active area can be increased, the greater factor of safety appears to take care of occasional variations. Consistency in golf depends entirely upon the presence in the swing at all points of an ample margin for error.

I think there can be no question that the golf stroke ought to be dominated from first to last by the left arm. This member is at the same time the guide and the controlling medium to apply the force derived from the rest of the body. It is hard for the average golfer to play an apparently right-handed game mainly with his left arm, yet he must remain an average golfer until he learns in a measure to do it.

Reverting again to Smith, except for the occasional lapse which Sargent first detected and I later, watching for it, saw, there is no finer left arm in golf than that of the Joplin lad. The arm is straight at address; it goes back straight in one beautiful sweep, and it comes down to the ball as straight as a poker. Simplicity is the essence of form in golf as in any other game, and Smith's method is as simple as A, B, C.

> But for controlled, accurate, and consistent hitting, the left arm simply must be straight when the clubhead meets the ball.

Watch the left arm always, but particularly on the short pitches. Whenever the stroke softens, there is great danger that the left elbow will flex. I like to have a feeling that the heel of my left hand presses downward upon the club as I strike the ball.

The most difficult part of this left arm business is to maintain it without taking away from the stroke most of its life and zest. To supply these qualities is the part of the wrists.

ON PLAYING BRITISH OPEN VENUES: CARNOUSTIE, HOYLAKE, AND ST. ANDREWS

The fact that the British open golf championship is to be played at Carnoustie this year—the first time at that famous old course—brings to mind a few comparisons and contrasts which may be of some interest.

In the first place, Carnoustie is a public course, just as St. Andrews is a public course, where anyone may play upon the payment of the proper green fee. St. Andrews particularly, I suppose, is often thought of as the course of the Royal and Ancient Golf Club, but as a matter of fact, the course is owned by the city of St. Andrews. The club makes a certain annual contribution toward the upkeep of the links, and in exchange its members have allotted to them certain starting times between specified hours in the morning and afternoon. At other times, it is entirely a matter of first come, first served. Of course this seems strange over here, where all of our championships are played over private club courses.

St. Andrews, on the other hand, is the least obvious course in the world. It is covered with concealed rolls, bunkers, hollows, and hummocks, which become more and more bewildering as the ground becomes harder.

14

Carnoustie is a very long golf course, requiring under normal conditions a good many second shots with the long irons, the spoon, and the brassie. Of course, if the ground becomes hard, this condition is greatly modified, but the course is very little easier because there are many cross-bunkers in front of the green, which makes the approaching difficult indeed when the greens dry out and become hard and fast.

Last Five Holes Like Hoylake

Some of the holes at Carnoustie, because they require some "big hitting," remind me very much of the five finishing holes at Hoylake, particularly the fourteenth, fifteenth, and sixteenth at the latter course. The last five holes at Hoylake probably foot up more yardage than any other five finishing holes in the world—2,288 yards, or a fraction less than an average of 458 yards to the hole. It will not be hard to convince anybody, I think, that if one is to make a score at Hoylake he must make that score in the first thirteen holes, because no man living is likely to pick up many strokes in those last five.

In this respect Hoylake and St. Andrews are a good bit alike. At Hoylake, it is a question of doing something in the first thirteen holes, and at St. Andrews, in the first twelve. These are the two courses in the British Isles which I like best of all, and they are the two which I think are exceptionally good championship tests. One queer thing is that St. Andrews becomes more difficult as the course dries out and becomes fast, while Hoylake becomes easier under these conditions, up to a certain point. The reason for this, I think, is that the golf at Hoylake is perfectly obvious. It is more like our American courses in that the fairways are quite clearly defined and the golf entirely straightforward.

St. Andrews, on the other hand, is the least obvious course in the world. It is covered with concealed rolls, bunkers, hollows, and hummocks, which become more and more bewildering as the ground becomes harder. When St. Andrews is fast, an immense amount of local knowledge is needed.

I think probably if we were to select the five finishing holes on these two courses for a comparison, we might decide that the finish at Hoylake was a bit tougher than the finish at St. Andrews, although I believe it is possible to get into more costly trouble on the old course. But I think if we put in the thirteenth hole at both places, that this would about swing the balance in favor of St. Andrews in the matter of difficulty: I have had several experiences, after turning the "loop" and passing the twelfth hole, of setting out for home against a strong breeze blowing off the sea. And, believe me, it is no pleasant experience when strokes are dear.

At Hoylake, my observation is that while you may very easily finish with a flock of fives, you are unlikely to take more than that on any hole, while at St. Andrews the limitation often appears to have been removed in the last third of the journey.

On Concentration

Lindbergh said that the hardest thing he had to do in crossing the Atlantic was to keep awake. When you stop to think about it, that seems reasonable enough. It is not so easy to understand why the hardest thing a golfer has to do is to keep awake—mentally. I do not believe there is another sport that requires the uninterrupted intense concentration of the mind that is demanded of a golfer in competition with others of anything like equal skill. In all other games, it is possible to take breathing spells without risking too much. But in golf, the unexpected can and usually does happen with such startling suddenness that the unwary person may be caught before he knows it. One lapse of concentration, one bit of carelessness, is more disastrous than a number of mechanical mistakes, mainly because it is harder to bring the mind back to the business at hand than it is to correct or guard against a physical mistake, recognized as soon as it appears.

A Wrong Impression

Nothing could be further from the fact than the fond notion that an expert golfer plays entirely subconsciously, without having to resort at all to conscious control. The habit of correct swinging causes a great many of the movements of the swing to be instinctive. But there are always two or three

17

things that have to be looked after actively, all the time. When this is appreciated, it is possible to understand what it means, when playing a first-class championship round, to concentrate upon the execution of seventy-two golf shots in a space of eighteen holes and over a stretch of upward of three hours' time.

And by concentration, I mean the kind that not only excludes everything foreign to the game, but also takes account of all that the player knows should be provided for. We find numbers of players with fine form who hit the shots as well as any one, yet fail to win because of imperfect concentration. It is so easy to walk up and hit the ball without thinking much about anything, and the player never realizes until the damage is done that he has not had his mind on the shot.

One particular instance—a single one of many I can remember—was a wide shot that I hit off the sixteenth tee in Augusta in the second round of the Southeastern open tournament. After starting with two shaky fives, I had regained the feel of the shots and was going along nicely. I had not mishit a shot since my second to the third green. In this state of affairs, I did what is the hardest thing to keep from doing—I began to feel secure—I went to sleep. Stepping onto the sixteenth tee needing three fours for seventy, instead of hitting a straight drive down the fairway, I hit merely a shot with a driver. I did swing the club, but I did not think. The ball sailed straight over the fence and out of bounds. The penalty gave me a six instead of a four.

Few and Far Between

The men who are capable of complete concentration throughout an eighteen-hole round can be counted upon the fingers of one hand. The others go to sleep on any number of shots. Sometimes they never realize, even afterward, that they did take a nap, and a lot of times they mistake fear and anxiety for concentration. It is possible to worry a great deal over the result of a stroke without really thinking of the way to play it successfully, and there are several different angles that may need consideration in trying to determine the correct way.

This is one of the ways that mental staleness is manifested when a player is overgolfed. The lack of mental alertness, which results, renders it impossible for him to maintain complete concentration on the details necessary to be considered for the different shots he is called on to play. He is trying to the best of his ability, but the thing is just beyond him, and he pays for it in the form of extra strokes on his score, or holes lost which might have been saved or even won with the right kind of keen mental application.

It might be asked again just what is concentration. I think that is very simple. There are certain fundamentals that go with every stroke. The right sort of concentration must take these into account. For example, the golfer should know that he should let the weight go with the swing. He should know also that he should let the left side come well around. These are two things he should think about in advance of the swing, especially if he is troubled with a fault of overlooking these two points. He cannot take them for granted; they must be thought out before he starts his swing, and he must think through the swing to see that they are carried out, or at least concentrate enough to see that they are started on their way. I mention these as just two examples out of several.

1930 ST. ANDREWS AGAINST JIMMY JOHNSTON

I once heard of a man who, playing in the final of a club championship, won his match on the last green after being 2 down and 3 to play. To accomplish this, he played the last three holes in 5-4-5 against a par of 4-3-4. After the match he was congratulated most heartily upon his magnificent victory—snatching victory from defeat by a courageous finish.

Some weeks later during the same season, this same man over the same course reached the final of an invitation tournament. This time, instead of 2 down and 3 to play, he found himself 1 up with 3 to play. He played the last three holes in par, 4-3-4, a stroke a hole better than on the previous occasion, yet this time he lost on the last green. Where his 5-4-5 had made him a hero, his 4-3-4 left him disgraced, a creature of no backbone who faltered under the fire of competition.

> Sensational recoveries and tragic
> failures are almost always accomplished
> by the cooperation of the two sides.

And so it goes in golf. I have, for this very reason, an unspeakable aversion for the word "guts," as it is so often used in describing an attribute of a golfer. Not only has the ability to finish well, or to play golf at all, for that matter, nothing in the world to do with physical courage, but it will be found that sensational recoveries and tragic failures are almost always accomplished by the cooperation of the two sides.

Such Estimates Unfair

In the recent British amateur championship at St. Andrews, my match with Jimmy Johnston was a case exactly in point. When we stood upon the fourteenth tee, I was 4 up with 5 to play. The match ended on the last green, where I won by one hole. Had I missed a six-foot putt there, we would have gone into extra holes, and had I eventually lost, I should have been accused of unspeakable things. As it was, it was said that with a comfortable lead I had "faltered unaccountably."

Let us see just how unfair such an estimate was to me, and particularly to Jimmy, who had made a really great finishing fight, and also let us remember that in nine cases out of ten, the imputation of a lack of guts is equally unfair.

The fourteenth at St. Andrews is over 500 yards in length, and on that day the wind was against Johnston's third shot of almost a hundred yards, but which finally lay four feet from the hole. My second, not a bad one, was forty yards short of the green. Jimmy's hole, 4 to 5.

At the fifteenth I really did make a mess of things, finally taking three putts to lose the hole. The sixteenth, 350 yards, we halved in well-played 4s. That left me dormie two, with the treacherous road hole coming up. Few people are crazy enough to play for this green, and neither Jimmy nor I were, on this day, among those few. We were both short, he with the better position. Needing only a half to win the match, I could take no chances with the road bunker and so rolled the ball to the middle of the green. Jimmy played a lovely run-up stone dead, so another hole was gone. The eighteenth we halved in 4.

Consider Other Player

Against Johnston I played the last three holes, 4-5-4, and lost one hole. Against George Voigt the next afternoon, I played them in 4-4-4, one stroke better, and gained two holes, a net gain of three holes and only one stroke.

Whether we regard a match of this kind as a triumph for the man who comes from behind, or a failure for the one who fails from in front depends only upon the point of view that we prefer to take. But in any event, we should be a bit more charitable with both than is the custom. Let us not place all the blame upon the shoulders of the loser without giving just credit both to him and his conqueror for the game the other man played. And, above all, do not sneeringly accuse him of having nothing behind his belt buckle. Try to place yourself in his position and frankly estimate if you could have done better.

ON STARTING THE
GOLF SEASON AGAIN

The most trying time of the year for the golfer is always the time when he comes out of hibernation and begins to try to tune his game back to a point where he can again enjoy it. After a long winter layoff, each club feels like a broomhandle, and each ball when struck transmits a shock up the shaft which makes the player think he has hit a lump of iron. Golf is not much fun during this period, but it is a thing we must endure to enjoy the pleasures beyond.

Any man would be grateful, I believe, for any hints which would help him to get through this "tuning up" period with as little suffering as possible. While all of us do not have the same troubles and have to apply the same correctives when we are playing more or less regularly, I have noticed that, at least the people with whom I play, manifest much the same tendencies when suffering from lack of practice. Apparently golfing muscles lose a great deal in elasticity and responsiveness when not in use, and these, unaccustomed to perform such functions, act upon demand in very much the same way for all individuals.

Lengthen Backswing

The first failure is in the length of the backswing. It is not hard to detect, in any case, a tendency to shorten the backward motion and whip the club back to the ball almost before it has reached the shoulder position. This is one way in which lack of assurance is manifested, the player being actually

23

afraid to let himself out as far as he would if extended to mid-summer form.

The second failing in part results from the first, although it is attributable also to the fact that the winter layoff impairs the player's sense of timing. This sense is entirely dependent upon practice, and when one fails to practice, he must lose the rhythm of the stroke. But it will be noted that in the spring the error is always on the fast side. No one ever swings too slowly.

Any man would be grateful, I believe, for any hints which would help him to get through this "tuning up" period with as little suffering as possible.

The third common tendency is to attempt to lift the ball instead of striking it firmly downward. This, I think, is due to a slack left hand and wrist. The player is not quite certain that he has done everything correctly, and he reaches the ball with the feeling that he perhaps ought to turn back to try it over again. He then either slackens his grip or "pulls" the punch and spoils the shot.

Watch for Faults

These are not all of the sorrows encountered during the first few rounds of spring, but they are those most commonly experienced. If we could start out on the lookout for them and promptly put them away, our days in purgatory would be lessened considerably. Let us resolve, then, that in the coming spring we will swing back slowly, that we will swing back far enough—even farther than we think necessary—that we will grip firmly with the left hand, and that we will punch briskly through the ball. If we will do and remember these few things, it won't be long before we will find the groove.

> But it will be noted that in the spring the error is always on the fast side. No one ever swings too slowly.

My own experience each year is somewhat tantalizing. From the end of the amateur championship until warm weather comes again, I usually play only three or four rounds, sometimes with as much as two months intervening between successive attempts. On these occasions, I go out relaxed and with very little concern about the results I am able to obtain. Then, I play fairly well. But when spring draws near and I begin to play a bit more often, I find myself doing the very things I have mentioned above. The first round, when nothing much is expected, is not so bad, but after that the trouble begins.

COURAGEOUS TIMIDITY

The more one thinks about golf and worries with the problems of the game, the more definitely it must appear that patience is the virtue in every respect to be most highly commended. Sometimes we call it by other names. Sometimes we attribute success to hard plugging determination, to intense concentration, to courage, and to steady nerves in a pinch. But always we have to admit that it is the conservative person who can keep going in an even sort of way, waiting until his opportunity arrives, who will in the end be judged to possess the other qualities we admire.

I think it was J.H. Taylor who made the statement that all of the great golfers he had known had been possessed of a quality which he chose to call "courageous timidity," a most happy phrase, for it expresses exactly the qualities which a golfer, expert or not, must have in order to get the most from whatever mechanical ability he may have. Courageous, to keep trying in the face of ill luck or disappointment; and timidity, to appreciate and appraise the dangers of each stroke, and to curb the desire to take chances beyond a reasonable hope of success. There can be no doubt that such a combination in itself embraces and makes possible all the other qualities which we acclaim as part of the ideal golfing temperament for the championship contender as well as the average golfer. When we have pronounced Taylor's phrase, we have said it all.

Golf is not a game of exact mechanical precision. Even the most accurate player in his most effective form must allow himself a certain latitude in playing any kind of stroke. How much this margin ought to be depends, of course, upon the skill of the player and upon how likely he is to make an error. What would be a risky shot for one, might be conservative for another. This means that each should know his own limitations and not rush in, in foolish confidence, to attempt things beyond the reach of his actual ability. Golf is said to be a humbling game, but it is surprising how many people are either not aware of their weaknesses, or else reckless of consequences.

What I particularly commend in a golfer is the patient waiting for opportunities. When playing either match or medal competition, I have found it always best to be conservative. In other words, I never attempt to cut a dogleg hole too close, nor to play a second shot straight on the pin when the hole is cut quite close to a guarding bunker. I always prefer to give myself as wide a margin as practicable, driving safely away from trouble even though it makes the second shot longer, and playing as close to the hole as I dare, but always remembering that the important thing is to be on the green. Once there, I never go too boldly to hole a long putt, but try to lay it dead, waiting for a birdie until a second shot drops near enough to eliminate the danger of taking three putts.

> Golf is not a game of exact mechanical precision. Even the most accurate player in his most effective form must allow himself a certain latitude in playing any kind of stroke.

One of the difficult things in the game is to maintain this waiting attitude when the start is bad. A few strokes or a few holes lost at the very beginning often causes a man to blow up completely. Feeling the loss, he is impelled to try to retrieve the strokes or the holes immediately. He tries things he can't do; takes foolish chances trying to beat par. A few of these fail, he finds himself going from bad to worse, soon becomes desperate, and finally goes all to pieces. Any of us have seen it happen in just this way, time and time again. We have probably realized then the mistake the poor victim was making, but we failed utterly to read the lesson to ourselves. Just because three holes in a row have been lost, it does not follow that the next three must be won. Rather, stop the tide and hang on by consistent sane play, picking back a hole here and a hole there as your opponent slips, or when a favorable break turns your ball up within holing distance. A good steady pressure kept on an opponent will win back holes quickly enough, when they start to come.

Mistakes Are Made

A player of any class must realize that some mistakes must be made. He must not permit them to disturb his balance. A bad start may be discouraging, but it should be remembered that extra strokes are no worse on the first hole than on the last. I always like to hear a fellow say: "Well, I'm glad that's done and behind me."

THE ESSENCE OF GOLF'S ENJOYMENT

Rex Beach writes humorously, "I have made a discovery lately. Golf is a game only to the dub; he alone gets any fun, any satisfaction, and perhaps any great benefit out of it. To the man who is seriously afflicted with it, to the so-called good player, it is a torment." It is difficult to deny that Mr. Beach touches the very soul of the game, as he goes on to describe the joy of the cherubic duffer celebrating his first score under a hundred, and the misery of the club champion who has putted badly to amass a wretched total of seventy-seven. The whole thing is ridiculous, we must admit, yet it is golf through and through.

The philosophy of the confirmed duffer, of the man who enjoys golf because it is a game that takes him into the air for exercise and congenial company, and who cares not how he plays it, is most admirably epitomized in a few words of a friend of mine who said, "We have never mastered golf until we realize that our good shots are accidents and our bad shots, good exercise." What a fine philosophy to take out upon the course!

In a greater or lesser degree it applies to us all, for no matter how expert we fancy ourselves to be, we can never make a score or play a round which, if we are honest with ourselves, we can mark up to our entire and individual credit. The best players in the world are to a large extent the playthings of luck or "accident"; numbers of their fine scores are attributable in some important detail to the fortunes of the game. Yet we all grumble about a putt that switches out of the hole, and think nothing about a lucky bounce that carries the ball away from a bunker which might have exacted a toll of many strokes. The breaks in our favor we accept as being as they should be, and remember only the untoward happenings.

Always Find Suitable Rival

The real dub enjoys golf because he plays it with due respect to his own limitations. It is difficult, sometimes, for the more favored ones to comprehend how it is possible for a man to enjoy compiling a score of a hundred and thirty or more. They know very well that if they ever played such a round, they would throw their clubs away. But the whole thing is comparative, and it matters not how terrible a golfer may be, he can always find someone who can give him an even game. And they can whoop and howl together over the funny shots, and mutually admire occasional successes.

> "We have never mastered golf until
> we realize that our good shots are
> accidents and our bad shots,
> good exercise."

Yet, speaking seriously, it is unfair to say to the so-called good player, "Golf is a torment." The one thing that kills the chances of the good player to enjoy any sort of a round is that his play has become reliable enough for him to set himself a standard. I remember one day at East Lake some time ago, when Frank Ball had just arrived to take up his duties as professional. One of the members had taken one lesson from Frank, and on this day he was holding forth in the locker room on the capabilities of Frank as a teacher. "Why," he said, "I have had only one lesson from him and it has taken twenty strokes off my game." I knew at that time that the fellow had not yet beaten a hundred, so I wondered what figure he had established as his "game." The fact is, I suspect, that his game varied so much from day to day that he did not know what it was. That is one of the big reasons the dub can enjoy his playing. He can never be disappointed.

A Philosophic Mind Needed

I have been myself, ever since I can remember, clearly one of those poor unfortunates who has taken the game seriously. I have suffered the anguish that Rex Beach describes when I have messed up a few holes and finished with a score in the high 70s. The dub cannot understand how such a score can be considered bad. He does not know that comparatively, the difference between 72 and 77 is far greater than between 110 and 130.

The great trouble with all of us who grumble and swear over the game and spoil an otherwise pleasant afternoon with congenial friends is that we do not understand the game nor ourselves. In this we could take a number of lessons from the dub. For, no matter how good we may be, if we should fancy that we have mastered golf to the extent that we can go out, day after day, and play as we please, then we are bigger fools than ought to be left at large.

PITCH FROM THE ROUGH

When a ball is played with a mashie or mashie-niblick from rough grass or from a heavy lie on the fairway, it can be safely predicted that it will have plenty of run left when it hits the ground. If we add to the condition of the lie the further circumstance of a strong breeze directly at the player's back, the run is unavoidable. It seems to me that if the average person could appreciate the difficulty of stopping a shot under these conditions, he would be not only less critical of the expert, but more saving of his own strokes. Pitch shots from long grass offer no particular difficulty as far as elevating the ball is concerned. The trouble comes in applying control and in making the ball stop where we want it.

Following Breeze a Hazard

First, it ought to be made clear why this sort of shot is hard to stop. The following wind itself is a hazard, even though the ball is lying well, where it is possible to obtain a clean gripping contact between the ball and the club. The currents of air moving along in the same direction in which the ball is flying do not offer as much resistance as calm air or as a breeze against the shot. Whatever resistance is offered is not sufficient for the spin of the ball to produce the climbing trajectory characteristic of a quick stopping. A good many people probably were surprised to learn that Walter Hagen at Muirfield last year played every one of his downwind shots as low as possible. He did this because he knew that a high shot thrown up anywhere near the green, with the strong wind behind it, might bound and roll to almost anyplace.

Contact Needed for Backspin

The effect of a heavy lie is to destroy whatever chance the wind may have left. The first requirement to produce any amount of backspin is that the club face secure some sort of grip upon the surface of the ball. As has been explained many times, the spin is produced by that part of the force of impact which is exerted tangential to the surface of the ball, as distinguished from that part which penetrates toward the center and propels it on its way.

> Pitch shots from long grass offer no particular difficulty as far as elevating the ball is concerned. The trouble comes in applying control and in making the ball stop where we want it.

That this tangential force may be appreciable, there must be a clean, dry, contact between club and ball, so that the club may grip the ball and impart spin to it. Anything which interferes with this contact lessens the chances of backspin.

Referring particularly to the shorter shots, it is best here to select a well-lofted club and to attempt to cut under the ball. This is one of the very few times when anything like a lobbing shot should be attempted, and it is the one time when there should be no effort to strike downward upon the back of the ball in the manner accepted for playing an ordinary pitch from the fairway.

But the most important thing is to avoid any silly idea that perhaps, just this one time, the shot will stop. Allow plenty of margin for the run of the ball and do not attempt to cut the bunkers too close. If there is any trouble near the green, the center of the putting surface is the best target to select.

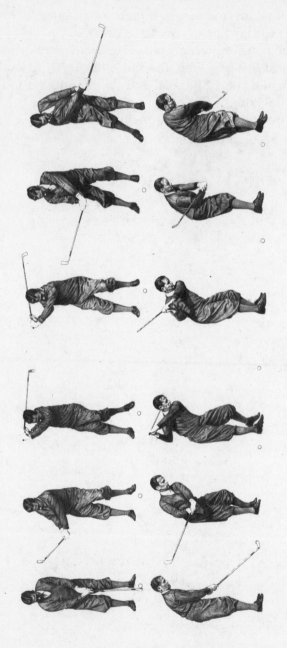

PROPER WEIGHT SHIFT

Sometimes in golf it is the little things the player does that throw him on or off his stride. As anyone knows, it does not take much to spoil a shot where a fraction of an inch or an almost infinitesimal instant of time may be the difference between success and failure. This applies not only to the execution of the stroke, but also to all the preliminaries which are necessary in order for the player to set himself for the stroke. Let one foot be the least bit away from its accustomed position, or the least variation creep into the grip, and the player at once begins to feel uncomfortable. Many times he does not know what is wrong. As little as the ordinary player knows about such things, the expert player attaches considerable importance to the way in which he approaches the ball. Anyone watching the play in an important championship will many times see the player addressing the ball and, apparently at the point of beginning his stroke, turn suddenly and walk away in order to begin the thing all over again. This action is usually attributed to temperament or to annoyance at some sound or motion. More often than not, however, it is an attempt to get set in a comfortable position before hitting the ball. The player's position at address is one into which he falls naturally, and when occasionally he feels that he is not quite at ease, no amount of shifting and twisting does any good. It is then, if he is wise, that he will turn away and take a fresh start.

37

Difficulty in Shifting Weight

One of the great troubles which the less expert player experiences is an inability to shift his weight properly. A great many start with most of the weight upon the left leg, a position from which a proper use of the body is impossible. Another mistake often made is addressing the ball too far back off the left foot, the player being in front of the ball in such a relation to it that the power of his body cannot be exerted behind the stroke. It is my suggestion that both of the difficulties can be aided by approaching the ball in the proper way.

Getting a Routine

The close observer will note that almost all of the first class players take their stances in substantially the same way. The procedure is about like this: they walk up to the ball, always from behind it, or from the left side in the case of a right-hand player. One look at the objective, and the club is placed behind the ball, the player at this time standing somewhat behind the line of the ball; then the left foot swings forward into position, and the body settles naturally in its place. After this, it is rarely necessary to move the right foot.

What Procedure Accomplishes

This procedure accomplishes several things. First, it fixes the distance from the feet to the ball in the best of all ways, by accommodating the distance to the comfortable extent of the arms and club. Personally, I cannot imagine taking my stance without first having some measure of this distance. The second advantage is that the player has approached the ball in the normal relaxed posture of ordinary walking. Approaching the ball from behind, the player stops in a place where his body will be behind the shot, and he sets himself naturally with his weight properly distributed. After all this, if he insists on throwing his weight upon the left leg, he must be considered hopeless.

Anyone watching the play in an important championship will many times see the player addressing the ball and, apparently at the point of beginning his stroke, turn suddenly and walk away in order to begin the thing all over again.

It is hard to appreciate that anything apparently so unimportant should be of any aid in actually striking a golf ball. Most of the better players have observed the practice so long that they scarcely ever think of it. But just the same, one of this class will hardly ever be seen to approach any shot from the forward side, or to step over the ball into position.

THE PERFECT IRON SHOT

Iron play differs in one very important respect from wood play. In playing any iron, the degree of accuracy required is much higher. The problem is not to get as much range as possible, but to hit the ball as far as the hole and no farther. This feature makes it desirable, except in certain special instances, to hit a shot with backspin which will cause it to stop very quickly after striking the ground.

Where one of my earliest troubles with the driver was a tendency to hit the ball too much downward, one of the most persistent of my errors with the irons is a desire to hit the ball too much upward. It is strange, of course, that this should be the case, for it would seem that whether my tendency were in one direction or the other, it would remain the same, no matter which club was being used. To understand why it does not, it is only necessary to take account of the different objects in view in playing the two clubs—the driver and the iron—one requiring roll, and the other a high quick-stopping shot.

Backspin Steadies Ball

Apparently, when one takes a mashie in hand to play a neat pitch to the green over a yawning bunker, his first impulse is to lob the ball high into the air. I have seen numbers upon numbers of duffers who attempt to obtain backspin in this way. They never stop to think that the lofted club was given them to enable them to secure the necessary altitude without this necessity.

Backspin is not merely a means of stopping the ball after it strikes the ground. It is also the agency which steadies the ball in its flight through the air, and holds it true upon the line to the flag. Anyone who has tried to pitch out of heavy rough, where it was impossible to impart swing to the ball, will be able to appreciate how much the spin adds to control. Played from a heavy lie, the ball often darts from side to side and may finish yards away from the line on which it started, and there is no way to foresee in which direction the shot will err.

> In the perfect iron stroke, the clubhead descends upon the ball and sends it on its way, passing afterward, still downward, until it strips the grass from the ground and rips a divot from the sod.

In playing an iron, and by this term I mean to include the pitching clubs as well, it is imperative that the player "stay down to the shot." That means that the left side of his body must not strain upward as he hits the ball. Left shoulder, left hand, and the clubhead must all stay down, and the weight of the body must have shifted with the stroke until most of it is borne by the left foot.

Correct Iron Shot Takes Divot

In the perfect iron stroke, the clubhead descends upon the ball and sends it on its way, passing afterward, still downward, until it strips the grass from the ground and rips a divot from the sod.

41

To show that this stroke is often misunderstood, I repeat a remark which was overheard among the gallery following Billy Burke and me in the Southern open several years ago. I had just played an iron shot from a cuppie lie to the seventh green when a man in the crowd was heard to exclaim, "I just can't understand how he can hit that ball so far when he digs up all that ground behind it."

It is important in iron play, in order to accomplish the kind of strike which I have described, that the left-hand grip should be firm and the left arm straight at impact. I also like to feel that I am pressing downward with the palm of my left hand.

ON JUDGING THE SLOPE AND SPEED OF LONG PUTTS

While two-hundred-odd struggling amateur golfers were trying to qualify at Brae Burn last year, Walter Hagen sat behind the eighth green with Grantland Rice. The eighth green at Brae Burn resembles the Atlantic Ocean on a windy day, with undulations running in all directions, offering treacherous slopes on a keen, fast putting surface which completely baffled the player who was not able to gauge their effect correctly. It was not so difficult to reach the green in one shot from the tee, but it was a trying ordeal to get down in two putts. Hagen could not have found a better place to make his study.

Apparently Walter could read in the faces of the men the degree of attention that they were giving to choosing the proper line to the hole. It was evident to him that the majority were too worried over the putting to give to the job the thought and concentration that it merited. The trained eye could readily see that many of the men who squatted composedly behind the ball, and went through the motions of studying the green, were really pausing in an effort to muster sufficient courage to hit the ball. Many of the expressions were totally lacking in indications that intelligent thought was being given to the problem at hand. Those who did appear to consider the hazards of the green were uniformly successful in getting the first putt respectably close to the hole. The others were likely to finish almost anywhere.

Train the Eye

All of which indicates that the first thing in putting to be considered is the slope and speed of the green. Many a good putter will advise you that he putts well because he follows through straight at the hole. Whether or not the follow-through is a virtue, it certainly cannot be a prime cause, for when it takes place, the ball has started on its way. I have never been a believer in a fixed putting style. It has always been my idea that more practice should be given to gauging the effect of a slope and to estimating the speed of a green; in other words, to training the eye, than to the mechanical perfection of the stroke. It is evident that no matter how accurately the ball may be struck, it is always necessary to select the line upon which it should be started.

Those who did appear to consider the hazards of the green were uniformly successful in getting the first putt respectably close to the hole.

As an indication that the line is the important thing, I can truthfully say that I have holed very few putts when I could not see definitely the path that the ball should follow into the hole. I have said before that sometimes this line seemed to be as clearly defined as if someone had marked it out with white-wash. I cannot remember failing at least to hit the hole when I have been able to see this line.

Line to Hole Often Obscure

In this connection, there is one thing a golfer should always remember and always practice. In any round there are always numbers of times when the proper line to the hole is obscure. If it were always visible, we should miss few putts. But it is always a good practice, when the correct line cannot be determined, to borrow generously from any slope and attempt to make the ball pass a tiny bit above the hole. If the ball remains above the hole, there is always a chance that it will fade into the upper side, and it is certain that it will, at any rate, stop not far away. But once a putt begins to roll below the hole, every inch that it travels carries it further from the objective.

The art of judging slope and speed is not entirely God-given. It is possible, to a great degree, to develop the faculty. But the major part of any putting practice should be directed to that, rather than to the development of a perfectly accurate stroke.

DEALING WITH EMOTIONS

In order to fully appreciate what one sees from the gallery at an important championship, one must have some idea of what is going on in the player's mind as he is compiling his score. The average observer is quite capable of understanding and appreciating fine play. He knows the mechanical difficulties of the game, which shots are good and which are bad, but rarely do we find a person who, never having competed himself, is able to experience with the player the nervous and emotional upheavals which in many cases ultimately determine the result. Although the accomplishment of such a thing is far beyond any powers which he may picture for himself, the average man is still able to admire and not wonder at the almost perfect rounds turned in by some of the leaders. But how one of these men, with apparent command of every shot, can suddenly break from a stride of perfect golf into a gait, about keeping step with lady's bogey, is wholly inexplicable to him.

How could anyone who has not played in an open championship find a satisfactory explanation for what happened to me at Olympia Fields or, still worse, to Roland Hancock in the same championship? I had scored 73, 71, 73 for the first three rounds, and was leading the field by three strokes. Beginning the last round, the first five holes were passed in one stroke under par. The course at Olympia is difficult at the start and at the finish, but fairly simple in between. So when I holed a

47

birdie 3 on the fifth green, I was in a particularly happy frame of mind, for I considered my troubles were over, at least until the fourteenth hole. But suddenly everything that had been going on smoothly began to go quite the other way. A five on the par 3 sixth hole was followed by a badly hooked drive which came to rest immediately behind an evil-looking tree. I am sure no one among the crowd could to any extend appreciate my feelings as I looked at that ball.

To those who had played enough golf to understand the possibilities of the situation, it appeared only that there must be a chip to safety, an iron to the green, and two putts for a five. That, with the five on the preceding hole, would wipe out the lead that I had at the beginning of the round, but unless someone became inspired, there was no chance of being worse than even with my closest pursuer.

> How could anyone who has not played
> in an open championship find a
> satisfactory explanation for what
> happened to me at Olympia Fields?

But one loses all sense of proportion in these golf tournaments. For the moment, the whole world seems to hold together only upon the hope of winning the championship. I saw immediately, instead of the five which should have been quite attainable, all the terrible things that might happen. I felt as though the bottom had dropped out of everything, and that there was just no need to struggle on. The prospective five turned into a six, and each of the next three holes I tossed away another stroke before I could recover any semblance of balance.

Possibly, it is just as well that the average person in the gallery does not appreciate the emotions to which the com-

48

petitors are subject; otherwise, we should all be regarded as utter fools.

Senseless though it may be, this panic or despondency plays a most important part in tournament golf. No player ever collapses because he forgets suddenly how to use his clubs. Sometimes the untoward incident which kindles the fire is trivial enough, but when aided by a vivid imagination, it quickly gains sufficient proportions to stampede the already overwrought nerves. To crack under the stress of such a condition is always humiliating to the player, and it lies not with anyone who cannot understand to censure him. Most of those who criticize would likely come off worse than he.

HALF OF LONGER CLUB VS.
FULL SHORT CLUB

One tantalizing thing about golf is that very often, the closer one gets to the green, the harder the next shot becomes. This is particularly true when the hole is placed close behind a guarding bunker and the green is firm enough to make stopping the ball difficult. In such a case, there is a distinct advantage on the side of the man who is far enough away to be able to hit a crisp, firm shot.

> Willie, being back far enough to play a firm mashie-niblick pitch, brought off a beautiful shot that dropped like a poached egg six or seven feet past the hole.

The first hole at Brae Burn during the amateur championship presented such a problem. A creek coursed across the fairway some thirty yards short of the green, and along its banks for several yards back the grass was long, and the lies heavy. It was virtually impossible to control so short a pitch from the heavy grass. Almost every man in the tournament used either a spoon or an iron off that tee, not entirely, as many supposed, to avoid driving in the creek, but to make the second shot easier by adding some forty or fifty yards to its length. The hole was not especially difficult, so it was a simple matter to hit a firm mashie-niblick shot boldly up to the flag.

When Willie Macfarlane and I arrived at the eighteenth hole of our first playoff at Worcester, after Willie played his second shot, I was left in about the most uncomfortable position I can remember. The hole is approximately 350 yards in length, the green protected by deep bunkers entirely across the front. The hole on this day was cut a scant fifteen feet beyond the bunkers, and the green was unyielding. Whether by design or not, Willie's drive on this hole was very short, stopping just short of the crest of the slope over a hundred yards from the green. Mine was much longer, and stopped about forty yards short of the cross bunkers. Willie, being back far enough to play a firm mashie-niblick pitch, brought off a beautiful shot that dropped like a poached egg six or seven feet past the hole.

Whenever it becomes necessary to drop the ball dead upon the green, it is always better to press the shorter club than to spare the more powerful one.

After that shot, I had to abandon the plan which I had conceived of pitching safely onto the green to take my chances in the putting. Macfarlane was likely to hole his putt, so that a four for me would be one stroke too many. The only shot that had a chance of success was too dangerous to try without considerable fear. But I had to lay my niblick back and attempt to "cut the feet from the ball." I hit the shot a bit heavy, but the ball struck at the end of the bunkers and struggled up barely on the green. That was by far the most difficult shot I have ever had to play at a crucial moment in a championship. Later that day, at the same hole, I dropped my pitch so definitely into the bunker that the ball could not wiggle through, and so lost the championship.

A fine thing for anyone to remember when confronted by a shot of this kind from any distance is that the more firmly the shot can be hit, the more likely the ball is to stop. Many players do all pitching with the mashie-niblick, without respect to the nature of the shot. It is virtually impossible for them to hit firmly from the shorter distances, and the same thing is true of the man who used a spade or a mashie for a shot which could be played with a more lofted club.

Whenever it becomes necessary to drop the ball dead upon the green, it is always better to press the shorter club than to spare the more powerful one. Often I play almost a full shot with a niblick instead of a more moderate stroke with some other club, simply because I know that I don't have to hit the ball so accurately in order to make it stop.

FINDING A KEY

Playing on the National Golf Links not very long ago, I happened to be driving very well. Alec Girard, the club professional, walking around with us, asked if there was any one thing I thought about that enabled me to keep on hitting the ball where I wanted it. I replied that when I was hitting the ball well, there were always one or two things which I made certain of doing, and the doing of them would assure success for a while. But they were not always the same things. One conception was good for only a limited time, and when the charm wore off, I would have to begin looking for something else. Alec said emphatically that his experience had been the same.

> The stance can vary considerably, shifting the feet to favor a hook or a slice; the ball can be shifted about within ample limits with respect to the feet.

This is one of the things that our theorists and analysts overlook when they are not themselves reasonably capable players. It is of great value to have a clear understanding of the successive movements which make up a correct golf swing. This much is needed in order to enable one to recognize and correct faults as they appear. But no human is able to think through, and at the same time execute, the entire sequence of correct movements. The player himself must seek for a conception, or fix upon one or two movements on which to concentrate, which will enable him to hit the ball. And then, when this wears out, because, perhaps, he begins to exaggerate or overemphasize it to the detriment of something else, the search must begin anew for another idea that will work. In this process there inevitably are alterations in the swing, not in fundamentals, of course, nor of radical proportions, but more than can be accounted for in any series of diagrams.

If the expert player, possessing a swing that is sound in fundamentals, has to be continually jockeying about to find the means of making it produce fine golf shots, what of the average golfer who has never developed such a swing? Still groping for some sort of method that will give him some measure of reliability, it is only natural that he should try almost anything. If he ever wants to improve, he must strive in every way possible to build up a sound style.

Tinkering

There is a whole lot in knowing what to monkey with, and what to leave alone. In making day-to-day adjustments, I never consider even for a moment making any alteration, however slight, in my grip. It is of the utmost importance that the hands should be placed on the club so that they can perform certain necessary functions, and the correct grip should be the first thing learned. But after this has been done, the accustomed feel of the club should never be altered. It is only through the grip that the player is able to sense the location of the clubhead and the alignment of the face. If he is constantly changing here, he cannot possibly retain this feel. The temptation is great sometimes to correct a temporary hooking or slicing tendency by shifting the right hand more over or under the club. This should never be done. If the grip is wrong, change it by all means, but let the change be a permanent one.

The stance can vary considerably, shifting the feet to favor a hook or a slice; the ball can be shifted about within ample limits with respect to the feet. These little changes are by no means fundamental. Even what might didactically be prescribed as the correct swing allows some latitude in these matters.

> If the expert player, possessing a swing
> that is sound in fundamentals, has to be
> continually jockeying about to find the
> means of making it produce fine golf
> shots, what of the average golfer who
> has never developed such a swing?

The important thing which the non-golfing theorist or analyst can seldom appreciate is the importance of the player's conception of how to put the correct swing to work. Very often, what a man feels that he is doing is more important than what he does. The feel, the experience, is so much easier to remember and repeat. When you arrive at a feeling of doing something in any part of the stroke, and that something continues to produce good results, you will have a player's conception to hang onto. It is something upon which to concentrate, and which everyone must have in order to play consistent golf. Even the soundest swing must have some simple control to keep it in order.

Edward F. Casper

SHORT SHOTS AND LONGER SWINGS

Playing the thirteenth hole at East Lake the other day, I had to play a pitch of about eighty yards over a bunker to a fairly hard green. The problem of stopping the ball near the hole was made somewhat difficult because the wind was directly behind the shot. I played the stroke with a niblick, swung the club well back, and happened to hit the ball exactly right. Indeed, I suppose I hit it too well, for the backspin brought the ball to a stop more quickly than I thought it would, and left it some fifteen feet short of the flag.

> Possibly he has had the virtue of "compactness" pounded at him too much.

One member of our match was standing nearby, waiting to play his own ball which lay some five yards closer than mine. As soon as I had played, he remarked that he had never noticed before how far back I swung my club in playing a shot as short as the one I had just made. I replied that I had been trying for years to lay particular emphasis upon the necessity of an ample backswing to prevent hurried hitting and to enhance the smoothness and rhythm of the stroke.

"All right," said he, "watch this." And with an effortless, unhurried swing he proceeded to flick his ball up four feet from the flag, well inside mine, and then holed the putt. He was positively beaming as we left the green. "You know," he said, "I have been playing those shots with a much shorter stroke and I have always tabbed them, or topped them, or missed them some way. When I took a longer backswing I knew I had plenty of time to hit, so I didn't hurry. It felt like the clubhead was doing all the work, and I just let it swing."

> "All right," said he, "watch this." And with an effortless, unhurried swing he proceeded to flick his ball up four feet from the flag, well inside mine, and then holed the putt.

And there you have one of the most important lessons in golf—important in connection with the playing of every shot from the full drive to the smallest putt. And yet it is appalling to see how many players attempt to go on without regarding it. Whenever you see a backing duffer playing a succession of jerky, nervous approaches, just think how much better he would look and how much happier he would be if he would only swing instead of chopping. His short backswing, which he instinctively realizes is not enough, causes him to yank his club down before it has really reached the top. His effort to make full use of every inch that he has allowed himself causes him to hurry and to upset hopelessly the balance of his body and the rhythm of his stroke.

Overswinging

Almost every average golfer worries about overswinging. Women players, with their weaker hands and wrists, are inclined to lose control of the club at the top of the swing, but the male player more often errs in the opposite direction. Possibly he has had the virtue of "compactness" pounded at him too much. At any rate, the common fault is a too abbreviated backswing. There is no good reason why, for a full shot, the club should not be swung back beyond the horizontal position. The added inches mean that much more space and more time to get going, and that tends to eliminate the jerks and to smooth out the whole process.

ATTITUDE

Although conditions of ground and weather do objectively affect the playing of golf, a great deal of the adverse effect is caused by the state of the player's mind. A hard wind or a heavy rain inspires in the player a feeling of combativeness or of desperation, and prevents him from going about his business in an equable frame of mind. He is tempted to strive to do a little bit more than he can—to hit a little harder, or to exercise closer control. It is only after a lot of experience that one learns that best results are reached by refusing to regard the elements except as a circumstance to be considered in deciding upon the character and direction of the shot. If we regard them as definite contrary forces which must be overcome, they become very powerful enemies in reality.

> Sometimes their dejection reaches
> the extent of complaint and protest
> against a situation which they can
> in no wise alter.

Walter Hagen furnished an outstanding example of what can be done by keeping and using one's head. It was in the second round of the open championship at Olympia Fields. Walter had gone out in 40 and played the tenth hole only of

60

the incoming nine when he was overtaken by a veritable torrent of rain, accompanied by some amount of wind. I had finished only a short while before the storm broke, and had reached the shelter of the clubhouse in time. Looking out from my window, I could scarcely see through the rain to the tenth tee, not over 100 yards away. I naturally thought of Hagen's situation. Out in 40, it seemed unlikely that he could better that figure coming home. An 80 for the round would substantially mean elimination.

Greens Play in Rain Easier

But Hagen did on that nine what no golfer in the world can do as well as he. He shut his eyes and his mind to the rain and wind. He thought of only one thing—of getting the ball into the cup—and came back in 33. I saw him afterward and asked him, in wonder, how he had been able to accomplish the remarkable score. He apparently wasn't quite sure himself— "just played golf," which after all is a pretty fair explanation.

> A hard wind or a heavy rain inspires in the player a feeling of combativeness or of desperation, and prevents him from going about his business in an equable frame of mind.

When there is only rain to contend with, without wind or unusual cold, the difficulty is almost wholly of the players' own making. Aside from slippery grips and water that trickles icily down one's neck, there is no reason why even a heavy rain, unless it inundates the course, should offer any insurmountable problem. The wet turf takes a few yards off the drive, but the play around the greens is made correspondingly more simple. Often it is a joy to putt on a soaked green, where every putt may be struck boldly for the hole.

Bad Conditions Sometimes Help

In 1922 at the Brookline championship, during the second qualifying round there came a deluge. When I reached the first green, the whole surface was covered with water, and it was necessary to putt with a mashie. Bernard Darwin, who came over that year as a member of the British team, had returned to the clubhouse, confident that the day's play would be thrown out. Playing fourteen holes in the rain, I was very pleased with a 72, a stroke better than I had accomplished the day before in the glorious sunshine. But Jesse Guilford, playing immediately behind me, turned in a 70, and Chick Evans, finishing some time ahead and hence playing the full round in the worst of the rain, finished in 74. The fact that all three of us had improved noticeably upon the scores of the day before, and there were many others who did likewise, is evidence enough that the downpour was not a serious handicap.

Many players who have a right to be rated above the average are quite happy with the game as long as conditions remain pleasant and normal. But a little wind or a drop or two of rain immediately throws them into such a panic that they can by no means do themselves justice. Sometimes their dejection reaches the extent of complaint and protest against a situation which they can in no wise alter. It is, of course, reasonable to expect that unfavorable weather will add a few strokes to the score in the end, but there is no reason to allow a call of a dozen or more.

Rub of the Green:
Lucky Bounces

One important reason for the uncertainty of golf is the fact that it is played over ground which in contour remains almost as nature shaped it. Hills and valleys, small mounds and undulations deflect the ball this way or that. Two balls striking within a foot of the same place may finish yards apart—one in a bunker, the other near the hole.

One is inclined to overlook the times when a few feet more or less meant a difference of several strokes. When a ball stops a few inches short of a hazard, we seldom stop to think how lucky it was that it failed to roll in. Things of that kind occur on almost every hole of the course. They are regarded as merely a part of the game. It usually requires something almost startling to awaken us to a full appreciation of the part actually played by the breaks of the game.

A Lucky Bound

The first championship I won was saved for me by my ball taking a bound toward the hole instead of away from it, as it might well have done. Playing the sixteenth hole at Inwood in the last round of the championship of 1923, I was in the lead but strokes were quite precious. After a good drive, I elected to play a number three iron to the green, which was protected by bunkers and mounds on either side, leaving a narrow

63

opening in front. I must have felt the strain, for I wheeled the shot off to the left of the green, barely missing the bunker on that side, and watched it scamper into the roadway, out of bounds. That meant the loss of stroke and distance, so I was playing four from the fairway.

Severely shaken by the mishaps, I came very near to duplicating on the next shot the mistake which had cost me dearly on the first try. I remember wondering, as I watched the ball in the air, what I should do if that one, too, should go out of bounds. The ball came down on the side of the mound at the front of the green and, bounding almost at right angles, came to rest not over ten feet from the hole. I made the putt, and so escaped with a five that ought to have been at least a seven. When I took six at the last hole, I was even more grateful for the lucky bound, which enabled me to tie Cruickshank and remain with a chance for the championship.

When a ball stops a few inches short of
a hazard, we seldom stop to think how
lucky it was that it failed to roll in.

When a fine drive goes sailing down the middle of the fairway, it is reasonable to expect that it will find at least a decent lie. But when a wild shot goes off into the woods or rough it is not likely to find an agreeable resting place.

Fortunate Lie for Hagen

When Walter Hagen and Leo Diegel came to the third tee on the No. 4 course at Olympia Fields one afternoon, they were all even after thirty-eight holes of play. They were playing a semifinal match in the P.G.A. championship. Diegel got away a fine drive down the narrow fairway. The course was fast, and he was left with a fairly easy second. Hagen, on the other hand, hit one of his wildest slices over a clump of trees and into what everyone knew was deep rough. Apparently that ended the thing as far as Hagen was concerned. The situation of the green was such that a shot from the position of Hagen's ball would be almost impossible if it were found in long grass.

Most of the gallery scampered over the hill, anxious to see what Hagen could do in the way of extricating himself from a bad situation. But on arriving there they found that Hagen was by no means out of the match yet, for instead of long grass, his ball had found a perfect piece of turf in a nursery which was kept to supply patches for the greens.

A fine iron shot put him on the green in two, and the hole was halved in four. Diegel was shaken by the surprise of that half, and topped his drive on the next hole. There was no nursery waiting for him, so Hagen won the match.

Whatever may be a player's skill, he must have luck to win a championship of any kind, at least he must have no bad luck; golf is still a game rather than a science, and a game it is likely to remain. Possibly the feature of uncertainty is the chief reason for its popularity among players and spectators alike. One can never tell when the thrills will come thick and fast.

ON THE CHIP SHOT

M any times I have heard it said that a chip shot should be regarded merely as an extended putt, and should be played with substantially the same stroke as is used in the putting. In general terms, the chip and the putt are parts of what we call the short game, but beyond that there is absolutely no relation between them. Each requires a different technique, and proficiency in one department by no means carries with it success in the other.

The design of the player, when chipping from just off the putting surface, is to place his ball in position where the putt which follows will be as simple as possible.

It is beyond all reasonable expectations that a person may hole a chip shot, so little will be gained by playing always for the hole. Naturally, if the ball can be rolled to the edge of the hole the putt will be simple, whatever the condition of the green, but there are times when a four-foot putt uphill is a far less annoying proposition than one of half that length across a keen slope. It is well to keep in mind that the success of the chip depends upon the success of the putt, and is not measured by the number of inches separating the ball from the hole.

There is nothing more trying than the playing of a medal round when one is chipping badly. To be continually struggling to get down in one putt after the chip shot is likely to undermine the staunchest determination. It is rare when a competitor plays even one round in which he has not a lot of chipping to do. If he is not adept at the shot, the question becomes merely how long good putting will stand the strain. Sooner or later the strokes will begin to slip away.

Use More Than One Club

I think it is a bad idea to use one club for all kinds of chip shots and short run-ups. Familiarity with the implements, of course, has its advantages, but it is practically impossible to secure a club that is effective from all distances and over all conditions of turf and terrain. It is far better to be able to play the shot with any club which may be indicated by the shot at hand, so that the proportion of pitch and run may be accommodated to any position of the ball or hole with respect to the edge of the putting surface.

Methods of Play

Nearly every successful golfer is a skillful player of the chip shot. Nearly all of them play the stroke with any club, and with each club in two distinct ways. In one case, where the green is not especially keen, and where the cup is set far enough back from the edge of the putting surface to accommodate the normal run of the ball, the shot is played with feet close together and the ball off the right foot. The ball is struck a straightforward blow and is pitched without spin, taking its normal roll to the vicinity of the hole.

In case the hole should be cut very near to the edge of the green, or if the green should be keen or sloping, the expert places the ball opposite his left foot and plays the stroke with the face of the club lying off slightly. Pinching the ball from the ground in this way, the spin imparted causes the ball to drag during the first part of its journey upon the green, and come to a stop after a gentle roll.

The first method requires considerably less delicacy and finesse and is always the safer shot, if a club can be found which is capable of making the shot in that way. Usually, but not always, a chip that requires spin with one club can be played normally with a club of more loft.

But there are times when a four-foot putt uphill is a far less annoying proposition than one of half that length across a keen slope.

I think crouching is the worst mistake the average person makes when playing a chip shot. You will observe any number of players who stand to the ball with feet wide apart and bodies bent far down, taking a grip upon the club at the very bottom of the leather. Such an attitude invariably produces a tenseness which destroys all chance of executing a delicate stroke.

On Staying Behind the Ball at Address

This inquiry comes from Oklahoma: "Sometimes when I step up to the ball, I feel that I am going to hit it well. When this happens, I nearly always get a good shot. But at other times I know that I am all wrong the moment I take my stance, and no amount of shifting seems to help me. Even though I place my feet and stand the same, there is still something lacking that keeps me from swinging correctly. Can you suggest anything that might help me?"

My first guess here, which I make with almost complete assurance that it is the correct one, is that this player owes the discomfort and uncertainty which he sometimes experiences to a tendency to creep ahead of the ball as he addresses it. When he stays behind it, the chances are that he will hit it well because he will find no difficulty in swinging through. But the moment he gets too far ahead, even though his stance and posture remain in other respects the same, he finds his ability to swing destroyed, and the inclination toward quick hitting immeasurably strengthened.

Few golfing faults are obvious. If they were, we should all be able to turn in a better average performance. But this particular fault would win my nomination for the most insidious of all. It seems such a little thing, that we are scarcely ever willing to give it proper attention when so many other things, seemingly more vital, are giving us concern. So we go on and on, from bad to worse, trying everything under the sun, without realizing that the trouble and the correction are so simple.

"Stay behind the ball," is a splendid maxim. Not because it is impossible to get the ball too far forward, but because an error on that side makes itself felt at once, while a mistake in the other direction may be overlooked indefinitely. I recall at least two occasions when, after struggling with an uncertain game through several important weeks, I have discovered that the location of the ball had been at the bottom of all my troubles. And worst of all, although knowing better, the discovery must yet be the result of pure accident.

For any full length shot with the woods or the straighter irons, say down to the No. 3 or 4, it is never safe to allow the ball to move further back than a point about opposite the left heel. Opposite the ball or instep of this foot is better for the driver and brassie, and a location slightly back of the heel can be made to work all right for the pitching clubs with which the arc of the swing is more sharply descending. But even with these clubs, I should set a limit at a point midway between the two feet.

> "Stay behind the ball," is a splendid maxim. Not because it is impossible to get the ball too far forward, but because an error on that side makes itself felt at once, while a mistake in the other direction may be overlooked indefinitely.

The effect of placing the ball too far back, if the mistake is not exaggerated, is to cause the player to hit too sharply with his hands. Instinctively he realizes, as his club approaches the ball, that he must throw the head in front if he is to hit the ball straight and get it up. There is a feeling of being cramped and tight, knowing that there is not enough room for the completion of a smooth swing. If the mistake is exaggerated, in addition to the quick hitting, a serious fault of body movement becomes involved. Being in front of the ball at the top of the swing, when the return to the ball gets under way, in order to keep from smashing the shot into the ground, and in order to keep his feet, the player must throw his weight back upon his right foot. The consequences of this performance are obvious.

So whenever that feeling of discomfort returns, turn entirely away from the ball, and begin all over again. And remember to stay behind it. Give your swing ample room to go through without too much manipulation. Remember that the ideal is to start the club swinging and let it go through unchecked.

On Short Putts

About the most maddening sound a golfer can hear is the guffawing laugh of some over-a-hundred expert in the gallery when a four or five foot putt wheels out of the hole. The sound is not pleasant when the missed putt shrinks to two feet or less, but in that case the player's resentment is less violent, because he himself feels that he very likely deserves everything he gets.

I have often wished that there were some way to impress upon these loud-voiced persons the real difficulty of a short putt over a fast green when anything of importance depends upon the success of the effort. But because the duffer never feels the strain of competition, and possibly also because he seldom bothers to putt or count the short ones, he cannot appreciate how it feels to be confronting a yard putt that simply must go down.

Carelessness Often Cause

A good many short putts are missed through nothing less than rank carelessness. The thing looks so simple that it is hard to view it seriously. Yet it will be observed that comparatively few very short putts are missed in the course of a friendly informal round. This would argue that tension and anxiety causes more misses than lack of care, and we might be convinced of that were it not for the diabolical perversity which every golfer knows to be inherent in a golf ball. A casual tap with the back of the putter is enough to hole any short putt when no one cares much whether it goes in or not, but once large issues are placed upon the result, two hands and a world of pains are required to steer the ball into the hole.

Fear of Another Miss

There is nothing as demoralizing as missing a short putt. I have seen, numbers of times, a man's entire game, from tee to green, entirely destroyed in the course of a few holes as a result of one little putt. One missed, the next one looks doubly hard; that cast away too, then the approach putts begin to stop all distances from the cup, applying the pressure with ever greater force. Soon putting becomes impossible and the player begins to force his long game, trying to place his second shots close to the hole so that he will have to do little putting. A rapid progression through these stages results, before long, in utter rout.

Take Shots Seriously

I do not need to recount the matches in important championships that have been turned by the missing of an almost infinitesimal putt. Every man who has played golf knows how quickly the tide may turn. For not only does the miss destroy the player's confidence, but it also inspires his opponent.

Long ago I learned that no putt is short enough to be despised. I have long since realized the folly of one-handed, back-handed, and all other kinds of disgusted efforts. When it matters at all whether or not the next stroke goes in, no matter how short the putt may be, it receives as close attention as

I am able to give. I always take a stance and address, even when the ball is lying at the very edge of the hole.

> But because the duffer never feels the strain of competition, and possibly also because he seldom bothers to putt or count the short ones, he cannot appreciate how it feels to be confronting a yard putt that simply must go down.

I shall never forget my feelings as I prepared to tap in my last putt at Columbus to win the American Open. The thing could not have been over three inches in length, yet I was in mortal terror lest I should strike the ground and fail to move the ball even that distance. It can be done, you know.

It is always best to remember that even the little ones count.

On Hot Streaks in Golf

Reaction is just about as familiar to the golfer as it is to
stock market, and it is one thing that no man can esc
It is because of the inevitable reaction that the first ro
leader rarely wins an open championship, that the qualif
medalist seldom survives in a match play tournament,
that an unusual first nine is often followed by a mediocre
ish. In some incomprehensible manner, there seems to l
been established a standard to which the best of them cc
back, no matter how rampant they become for a while.

Inspired flashes when every shot goes exactly to the r
spot are familiar to almost everyone. Even the rankest be
ner sometimes finds himself in a mood for playing his
best golf, when unaccountably he plays shots which for
on another day would be impossible. On some days, all
and twenty foot putts go rolling to the bottom of the cup,
suing an undeviating course for no apparent reason, save
in the player's mind there is the conviction that they wil
so.

The queer part of the thing is that the player has all
no control over this inspired feeling or over the reac
which follows it; or, rather, let me say, disregarding gene
ties, that I have no control over. It is usually said that a
round follows a good one because in the course of play,
player unconsciously compares his progress with that of
day before, and becomes anxious and tense when he falls

hind what he accomplished on the previous occasion. But I have played enough to discredit this theory, for even when I have no hope and little special need to equal the score of a previous round, I have still been able to keep up, even with a standard of play which I am entitled to regard as normal.

It is for this reason that I have always been suspicious of these streaks of extraordinary scoring. The loss occasioned by the reaction usually exceeds the gain made while the inspiration lasts. One of these periods arrived for me when I was competing in the British amateur at Muirfield in my match with Robert Harris. Poor Robert, I know, was as bewildered as I was, for putts were dropping from all corners of the greens. The next day against Jamisson, however, I putted much worse than usual and was beaten.

> One of these periods arrived for me
> when I was competing in the British
> amateur at Muirfield in my match with
> Robert Harris. Poor Robert, I know, was
> as bewildered as I was, for putts were
> dropping from all corners of the greens.

My best scores have always been made when I have run into these streaks in the midst of a round—late enough to permit me to get back to the clubhouse before I entirely regained consciousness. At Flossmoor in the Warren Wood Memorial, at Winged Foot in the first round, and at Pebble Beach, when I scored a 67 in practice, I got off to very bad starts, and only struck a fast pace toward the end of the first nine. The inspiration lasted to the end or so, nearly that long that day. On other occasions I have spoiled a fine first nine by trying too hard to protect the early advantage.

Walter Hagen is apparently less affected by experiences of this kind than any other player. Hagen can have scoring

sprees without bounding back further than his normal gait. Yet in at least two instances the reaction got him, too. At Skokie, in 1922, and at St. Anne's England, in 1926, Hagen opened up fine 68's in the first round, only to follow up with second round scores in the high 70's.

There is no accounting for things like this, except by invoking the old law of averages. The player feels as keen, and he apparently is hitting the ball well. But the second shots finish twenty feet away instead of five, and long putts look into the hole without dropping.

ON DEFEAT AT PEBBLE BY
JOHNNY GOODMAN

Since the finish of the Amateur championship at Pebble Beach, many people have asked me about my match with Johnny Goodman of Omaha, in which Johnny arranged for me a prompt exit from the competition. What sort of a player is Goodman? How did you feel? And what do you think of eighteen-hole matches? are some of the questions.

One must realize that a tournament match over the short eighteen-hole route, especially when the going is pretty close, affords very little opportunity to study the style and golfing capabilities of an opponent. While one is hoping secretly that some shot will go astray, and that some opening will be left, it is hard to detach oneself sufficiently to appraise fairly the merit of a swing. About all I observed was that Goodman is a very good looking golfer—compact and businesslike—a player who appears at every moment to know what he intends to do the next. The best part of his game against me was undoubtedly his play around the greens, where all chip shots were very close and every hole-able putt seemed destined for the bottom of the cup from the moment it was struck.

Has Good Temperament

Johnny is only 20 years old, but he showed a splendid temperament in that match, never permitting anything to disturb his composure. If he was ever nervous, it was impossible for me to detect the slightest trace. Throughout the entire match, he went about his business calmly and without unnecessary ado, always in a pleasant, friendly manner, but not with the garrulous friendliness which is such a nuisance on a golf course.

As for the match itself, I must say in all frankness—although I do not favor eighteen-hole matches in a championship if there is any fair way to avoid them—that it was not the eighteen-hole system which beat me in the match with Goodman. Johnny won because he played the better golf, and that after I had snapped out of a bad start and had drawn on even terms with him, a position which I failed to maintain or better, simply because of my own mistakes.

It seems to me beyond question that the result was determined by the play on the thirteenth and fourteenth holes. Losing the first three holes, I had won the fourth and sixth with birdies, lost the seventh through taking three putts, and won the eighth when Johnny required two shots in a bunker. Halving the next two, we reached the eleventh green with Goodman leading by one hole. There he holed a putt from the front edge of the green for a three, and I got one of fifteen feet for a half.

The twelfth, a short hole, I won with three when Johnny was bunkered off the tee. Then came the thirteenth; Goodman's drive was somewhat shorter than mine, and his iron shot, cut a bit, landed in a bunker to the right of the green. Having always been short on the hole, I determined this time to be up. My spade shot pitched over the flag to the far edge of the green and hopped into a sand pit, cut into a bank over the green. A bad chip out finally resulted in my jumping a stymie to save a hole which should have been won.

The Sad Seventeenth

But the fourteenth was even worse for me. Johnny's tee shot landed in the rough on the right, his second under a tree on the left. After a drive and brassie fifty or sixty yards short of the green, I counted the hole as good as won, for Goodman had no chance to reach the green on his third. He played an excellent running shot, which brought up some fifteen or twenty yards short of the putting surface. Then I did it! - taking the shot heavily and flopping the pitch in a bunker short of the green, where the ball buried. Johnny pitched beautifully to a yard from the hole, and won when I failed to get close from the bunker.

That about ended the story for me, for we halved each of the remaining holes in par figures. There was one more shot, however, which I shall always remember. It was Goodman's tee shot at the seventeenth. This hole is about 220 yards to a very small green, with the ocean beyond and to the left. It is by far the most exacting hole on the course. From the time that I lost the fourteenth and became 1 down, I had looked forward to the seventeenth as almost my only hope. The fifteenth, sixteenth, and eighteenth were all easy pars, and in the condition of my putting, I had small hope of picking up a birdie on either. But I figured that if Johnny was to give me a chance at all, it would be at the seventeenth. I don't know if Johnny guessed what was in my mind, but at any rate he gave me a complete answer.

Playing out across the sand, he hit the most perfect spoon shot I have ever seen—as straight on a line to the flag as one could imagine—and as it brought up seven or eight feet short of the hole, it was not hard to see that my contestant's badge would soon be merely honorary.

It was a good match—one of the kind you don't mind so much losing, especially to a lad like Johnny Goodman.

ON SLOW PLAY IN CHAMPIONSHIP VS. CASUAL ROUND

I cannot leave the subject of the Pebble Beach championship entirely without touching on one more point that struck me forcefully, and to which I have given considerable thought since leaving the scene of the tournament. In a sense, remarks which I am going to make may be taken as a criticism of Pacific Coast golf, and I hope it will be remembered that it is intended to be entirely constructive and friendly.

Several of the California dailies were quite outspoken in their criticism of Dr. Willing, the runner-up, for the deliberate manner in which he prepared for and executed his strokes, at least one of them even hinting that the deliberation was intentional, with the idea of upsetting his opponent. It is unnecessary for me or anyone else to come to the doctor's defense upon an accusation of that kind, but it is appropriate to call attention to the unfairness of the criticism on other grounds.

Coast Golfers Play Slowly

I saw Willing play only in the afternoon round of the final match, but during that round I saw him take no unnecessary time or make any unreasonable delays. It may have been that in this match he was making a particular effort to quicken his gait in order to avoid even the appearance of excessive deliberation. But even so, it is impossible to see that the doctor

could have been a bit slower than a number of other players from the Coast whom I have observed. Apparently it has become the accepted idea in this region that the importance of competition makes it necessary to devote four or five minutes to a shot which would be played without hesitation and probably much better in a practice round.

There can be no odium attached to slow playing when the motives of grandstanding and of upsetting an opponent are eliminated—and these can be entirely eliminated from this discussion. But whether rightly or wrongly, I regard it as a mistake, considering both the player's efficiency and the welfare of the game in general. Golf depends for its growth upon public interest, and competitions are designed to stimulate public interest. Nothing can be less entertaining to the spectator than to watch a golf match drawn out by minute examination of every shot.

The East has no doubt been particularly fortunate in having the example of Francis Ouimet, who, though never hurrying himself, is still a quick player. I can't help thinking, too, that those who saw Francis hole a fine putt on the last green in his match with Little were convinced that time is not always the essence of golf.

After all, the degree of deliberation that is considered necessary depends entirely upon the man who is playing the game. It is his business to play the shot, and he should never be required to play until he is ready.

Delay Should Be Short

Some situations which one finds on a golf course require some amount of study before the player can determine the best way to overcome the difficulty. But these are unusual. The vast majority of shots from the fairway are but repetitions of countless hundreds played before. At least to one familiar with the course, as all tournament contestants are, the decision should be a matter of seconds.

There is one very cogent reason why the older heads and more prominent players should make an especial effort to avoid unnecessary delay. That is, on account of the effect of their examples upon the youngsters coming along. Youth is naturally confident, at least in golf, and playing with assurance, is not as likely as the older man to quail at the difficulties of a shot.

Lawyers and Slow Play

Whenever I see a much considered shot go astray, I can't help thinking of the lawyer who had unsuccessfully defended a client charged with murder. The trial had been long and drawn out, lasting nearly a month, and the lawyer had made quite a lot of noise and stormed eloquently in his argument. Meeting a brother lawyer on the street a few days later, the case came up in discussion, and the lawyer asked his friend what he thought of his conduct of the trial. His friend replied, "Well, I think you could have reached the same result with a whole lot less effort."

More often than not, the first impression is the best. There is no man capable of hitting a golf ball with sufficient exactness to warrant concern about the minute undulations which a very close examination might reveal. If he can care for the difficulties which he can see at a glance, he will have done well enough.

ALISTER MACKENZIE

D r. Alister MacKenzie, noted golf course designer, has long contended that a golf course, in order to hold interest for any amount of continuous play, must offer adventure. His conception is that nothing is as tiresome as certainty, and he blames the plethora of prescriptive courses, where every shot is known and ordered in advance, for the prevailing tendency to regard the score, rather than the playing of strokes.

Dr. MacKenzie always points to old St. Andrews to illustrate what adventure on a golf course can mean. There, certainly, one does not have one's course from tee to green plotted by the man who designed the layout. A considerable amount of room is always offered off the tee to allow a player to attack his problem in a way that suits his own tastes. But the game is always full of surprises until one has made a real study of the course. It is a lasting thrill to be forever discovering new slopes and rolls and hazards, which do not at first strike the eye, but nevertheless are of immense importance in the correct playing of the hole. This is what the Doctor means by adventure.

The Old Caddie

A friend of mine, who has recently returned from a visit to St. Andrews, tells a story which illustrates even better, perhaps. Upon starting his round, he had been provided with one of the picturesque old Scotch caddies who are so much a part of the place. My friend said that he happened to be playing particularly well this day and his caddy was exhibiting an avid interest in his game. (He *must* have been playing well.) On each tee he would be told exactly where to drive, and on the way to his ball he would be instructed on the placing of the second shot to obtain the most favorable position for the approach.

> "Well, I been a-carrying clubs here for thirty-seven years and I never saw that bunker before."

This had gone on for some time when my friend hit one tee shot better than the rest, which delighted the old caddie's heart. It was a good long one, and the old fellow had declared that it was exactly on the proper line. They walked on down the fairway, with the caddy explaining all the while about the playing of the next shot and praising my friend's excellent drive. Finally, they topped a sizable knoll, and there, nestling serenely in a small bunker about the size of a wash tub, was my friend's ball. The old caddy was abject.

"Well, I been a-carrying clubs here for thirty-seven years and I never saw that bunker before."

That is the adventure of St. Andrews. Every hazard is not out in the open, where it can be plainly seen, and there are no lines of rough down either side of the fairway marking the area in which the tee shot must land. You size up your problem and you pick your own way to solve it. But you are likely to learn something surprising each time you play a hole. It is not a course one would like particularly well at first, because the unseen hazards and rolls are likely to be considered unfair. But, as Dr. MacKenzie contends, the adventure holds interest.

IN AND OUT OF TROUBLE

The problem which the golfer always has is to keep his anxiety over the success of the shot from tying his muscles into knots. It is to this extent that the mental attitude is important. Some situations met on a golf course are necessarily more difficult than others, but the difference between a good lie and an unfavorable one can be considerably lessened by putting down the tension. I know that it is easier to give this advice than to follow it. The point is merely that it is helpful to remember that indecision and worry do more harm than good, and that no matter what the difficulty may be, it is best overcome by a sound swing.

The art of recovering from trouble, of retrieving mistakes without losing important strokes, is perhaps the tournament golfer's most important possession. In almost any round a few shots will go astray and find either long grass or bunkers, and if even one stroke is lost for each mistake, a respectable score becomes a forlorn hope. But the really expert player seldom plays so severe a penalty. Time after time he will escape with no loss where the dub would lose not one, but three or four. And the difference is largely in the mental attitude.

The moment the average golfer attempts to play from long grass or a bunker or from a difficult lie of any kind, he becomes a digger instead of a swinger. The suggestion that additional power is required to cut through the grass or to blast through the sand tightens him up and causes him to forget that power is best obtained by free swinging. The expert player does not make this mistake. He hits hard when the occasion requires, but he does not tighten up. He employs the same body-turn, wrist cock, timing, and swinging as in playing from the fairway.

Heroic Measures

It does not happen often that a shot from a bunker near the green requires more than a comfortably full swing. A shot of the explosive type—taking sand behind the ball—is by long odds the safest method out; unless the ball is deeply buried in the sand, no heroic measures are needed. Yet in such a situation there is an inclination to widen the stance, to set the feet firmly in the sand, and to bash the clubhead into the sand behind the ball.

This is the average golfer's method, and he never gets very far with it. The expert player, although, of course, he would rather find his ball on the fairway, still is not frightened. He still must play a golf shot and he must swing the club, and he knows he must not make any of the extraordinary preparations by which the average golfer only increases the tautness of his muscles. He assumes an easy, comfortable attitude, swings the club back an ample distance, and delivers a well-timed and accurate stroke. And he swings through the sand and ball. It is surprising, sometimes, with how little effort a ball may be extricated from a nasty-looking place if the clubhead is allowed to do the work.

BALL POSITION

It is difficult to note, in the methods of expert golfers, any precise agreement in the location of the ball with respect to the feet as the stance is taken. Yet, in watching both the expert and inexpert variety, it is possible to say that the one common tendency for all is to creep ahead of the ball—that is, to play it too much off the right foot. I can remember no instance, or a mistake in the other direction, among players who had any conception at all of a proper golf stroke.

The best practice when playing a normal full-length shot without hook or slice seems to be to locate the ball approximately opposite the left heel, with hardly ever a variation of more than two or three inches either way. Not even the most accurate and consistent players will, even throughout one round, address the ball at precisely the same point on every tee. Their instinctive reactions are able to accommodate a little change backward or forward. But the tendency is to creep ahead a little more, and a little more, until the correction or adjustment needed is too great to be made in a smooth swing.

In ninety-nine cases out of a hundred the player himself does not discover what he is doing until some one tells him or in desperation, after failing with every other corrective, he pulls himself behind the ball again.

Just the other day I was playing with Errie Ball, young professional at Highland, N.C. Ball is a good golfer, and up until a few days before we played, he had been playing quite well.

Then, he said, he felt his game slipping away from him and found himself unable to hold on, although he recognized the symptoms and tried very hard.

On this day it was quite noticeable that he was creeping ahead of the ball in just the way I have described. He would fall into his natural position and then at each waggle of the club, his feet would move a little more, and a little more, forward until in hitting, he had to make an effort to yank the ball back on line in order to keep from driving it far out to the right. When he simply made himself stay put in a proper position behind the ball, before beginning his swing, he began to hit straight shots again.

I once read an article which attempted to show why the admonition to "stay behind the ball" was misleading. It cannot be misleading if it is understood to mean, as I have always explained it, that the player must stay behind the ball so that he can move into it as he hits. An efficient stroke cannot be produced when an effort is being made to develop power in one direction while the body is moving in another, and contrary, direction.

> He would fall into his natural position and then at each waggle of the club, his feet would move a little more, and a little more, forward.

To be more specific: if, at address, the ball is located too far back, or if, at the top of the swing, the weight of the body should be ahead, that is on the left foot, there must be a movement backward, or else a sharply descending, hacking blow must be delivered. On the other hand, if the ball is played to any degree forward, and if the player should "stay behind the ball" at the top of the swing, he will then be in position to swing smoothly through, accomplishing at the same time an even transference of weight with the stroke.

My advice to all is to get the ball in front, where one can swing on it, instead of placing it back, where it can only be chopped at. And watch this one thing carefully, for it is possible to make a mistake here without being aware of it.

ADDING LENGTH

We have all been told often enough that relaxed muscles and a rhythmic swing are two essentials for the execution of a successful golf shot. More particularly, these are the essentials of any stroke which is intended to drive the ball any considerable distance. Yet, how many times do we see this knowledge disregarded by players who ought to know better, when the exigencies of a particular situation suggest the desirability of a few extra yards.

Two Main Tendencies

There are two main tendencies that the average player exhibits when he wants to hit hard. First, he is impelled to widen his stance, and second, to place himself further from the ball where he has the feeling that he can really "swing on it." In most cases, too, he will plant his feet firmly in the turf in order to complete what he considers "setting himself" for the stroke. And then he slugs at the ball and wonders why he doesn't achieve the enormous shot he had intended.

If one will take the trouble to observe, he will notice certain things which are characteristic of all true swingers of a golf club. First, that the posture of the body at address is fairly erect and that the location of the ball is near enough so that there is no need to stretch out for it; second, that the feet are not separated so widely that the movement of the hips is restricted and that they are not rooted into the ground. The whole picture will be one of apparent ease and comfort, entirely free from strain of any kind. And this is the beginning of a swing which will get distance and control.

Spreading the feet to an abnormal span ties up the midsection of the body, so that the possibility of a free turn of the hips—a source of great power—is entirely removed. The golfer must maintain a perfect balance, but what he wants is a balance in motion, and not a firm planting which will resist strong and outside forces. Aside from wind pressure, he has only to balance his own movements and the forces he himself sets up, and the occasional necessity of bracing against a strong wind is small excuse for tying up one's swing eternally.

So, also, for the practice of standing a great distance away from the ball. What the spreading of the feet does for the hip-region, so do the extension of the arms and bending of the body for the muscles of the arms, shoulders, and upper back. The long drivers stand noticeably erect, and their arms are permitted to hang easily from the shoulders. They place themselves at the outset where they are able to utilize every ounce of power that it is possible to derive from an ample turn of the body.

I grant willingly that there are times when one must have just a little more length than he would feel like trying for normally. It is not a good idea to strive for the ultimate length off every tee, but it is a fine thing to be able to produce a few extra yards when they are needed. But this additional can never be had by stretching and slugging. On the contrary, it is obtained more easily by increasing the turn, and use of the hips and shoulders.

93

VIRTUES OF FIRM GREENS

In a letter that I have just received from the Research Committee of the United States Golf Association Green Section, the statement is made, "We believe that much of the difficulty in maintaining putting greens is due to excessive use of water. The greenkeepers and greens committees point out that they do this in self defense because golfers all want soft greens." I am asked to say how I regard the practice of keeping green surfaces soft, even soggy, looking at the question purely from the playing standpoint.

There can be little question that the great mass of golfers in this country prefer their greens very soft. Such a condition makes the play much easier for all classes of players, and is in great measure responsible for the fact that tournament scoring is uniformly lower over here than in seaside links in the British isles. The difference is attributable more to this factor than to the much talked-of seaside gales, which, after all, do not blow constantly.

I cannot say which induced the other, or which came first, but there is a close relationship between our two great American preferences, the one for placing our green-bunkering very close to the putting surfaces, and the other for soggy greens which will hold any kind of a pitch, whether struck with backspin or not. The close guarding in many instances makes a soft green necessary if the hole is to be playable, and the easy pitching, on the other hand, makes it necessary to de-crease the size of the target in order to supply any test.

I quarrel with both ends of this proposition, whichever is to blame. These together are the two reasons, I think, why our golf courses, in the main, lack the subtlety of British links, and why our golf does not demand the strategy or the intelligent planning which it should. In my opinion, a properly designed hole should impose a test upon each shot that the player has to make. There should always be a definite advantage to be gained from an accurate and intelligent placing of the tee shot, or a reward offered for a long, well-directed carry over some obstacle. This advantage or reward can only be in the shape of an easier and more open road for the second shot. And when we soak the green with water, we absolutely nullify the advantage which the design of the hole has held out.

I do not believe in forcing a run-up shot in preference to a pitch in every case. But when one goes to the trouble of placing a bunker across the left side of the green in order to force the tee shot toward the right side of the fairway, why de-stroy its effect by soaking the green so that any sort of pitch over the bunker will hold? Our expert players are in the habit of playing long iron and spoon and brassie shots bang up to the hole. As long as they can do this, no architect can expect them to worry much about placing the tee shots.

> There should always be a definite ad-vantage to be gained from an accurate and intelligent placing of the tee shot, or a reward offered for a long, well-di-rected carry over some obstacle.

It seems to me that the ideal green would be sufficiently soft only to hold a properly played pitch—and by "hold" I do not mean to stay within a very few feet. To carry out the intention of the designer, conditions ought to be such that a definite penalty should be sustained by the player who has played himself out of position.

> We believe that much of the difficulty
> in maintaining putting greens is due to
> excessive use of water.

In this connection, I think one of our greatest needs is a fairway grass or treatment which will make the ground in front of our greens more reliable. If the greens themselves are maintained in a firmer condition, the need must arise on occasions to drop the ball short of the putting surface, allowing it to roll the remaining distance. I know very few courses where this is possible without great uncertainty.

FORMING GOOD HABITS

I think it will be admitted that any average golfer would find himself able to improve if something could be done to give him one, or even a very few, things to think about when he is making a stroke. The complaint we hear on all sides is that the whole thing results in a confused mass of ideas, things to do and things not to do, uncertainties of both method and results. Behind it all, there is the realization that one must concentrate on something, but what that something is, the poor man could not tell to save his life.

Of course, it is not possible to suggest one detail of the stroke or swing upon which the attention should be fixed. Even the most accomplished players cannot so simplify the game, for an action or movement which may need direction today may function quite well tomorrow merely following its long-standing habit. If this be true of the expert, it is apparent how impossible it is to make any such suggestion to one who has no correctly formed habits to rely upon.

But proper concentration during a round of golf is intended to accomplish something different from the perfect execution of each stroke. Powers of concentration alone cannot make up for any vast deficiency of skill and bring a mediocre player up to the level of one who possesses more real ability. But while on their respective form and ability to make shots and keep on making them, a wide gulf separates the champion from the average golfer, still, in one respect,

their problems are the same when they start upon a round of golf. What each wants is a good round for him, and this leaves a comparison of their expectations entirely out of the issue. To make the round satisfactory, it need only have exhibited in a favorable light the skill that the player possesses.

It is surprising how easy it is to lose sight of the very obvious fact that in golf the all-important necessity is that the ball should be struck truly. It has often been pointed out, in connection with putting particularly, that the best judgment in the world and the most careful consideration of hazards and other dangers, are of little avail if the shot is not well struck. But to a greater or less degree, depending upon the skill and confidence of the individual, every golfer on earth suffers from this disturbance of his concentration, by influences entirely outside his own swing. I, myself, admit to equal guilt with the rest, although I have asked myself time after time if I derived any benefit from worrying about a hazard, once I had decided upon the kind of shot to be played.

Learn Through Practice

This is one of the reasons why the golf swing cannot be learned in actual play. No one can entirely ignore the responsibilities attendant upon the playing of any shot in a round of golf, the matter how unimportant may be the issue. Habits should be formed and instruction had on a practice tee, where there is nothing to think about but hitting the ball.

ON HOW TO GET A GOOD START IN AN IMPORTANT ROUND

The statement of Billy Burke's that he always made sure of doing certain things when playing the first few chip shots of any round is the result of a thought which the experienced tournament player regards as of paramount importance, but which the average golfer, playing his informal rounds, never once considers. To Billy Burke, competing against the best golfers in the world, a single stroke often may mean the difference between victory and defeat, and he is made to realize that the first shot of a round is of just as much importance as any other.

> My advice would always be to swing
> easily on the first few shots; to think
> more of placing the first tee shot down
> the fairway than of driving it a prodi-
> gious distance.

This matter of getting off on the right foot is of immense importance for more reasons than one. In the first place, it is a serious handicap to burden oneself at the very start with a deficit that has to be made up. In medal play, a par round is usually the player's goal and Old Man Par never makes a slip. If you give him a start of two or three strokes, those strokes will be awfully hard to get back. In match play, a good beginning is equally desirable. Any number of matches have been lost to an inferior adversary merely because he was given encouragement by gaining an early advantage. O.B. Keeler used to tell me, whimsically, that the best way to win an eighteen-hole match was to start off with six 3s in succession. I was never able to challenge the truth of that statement.

Discover Pitch of Game

In important tournament matches, a man feels entirely justified in spending fifteen or twenty minutes in warming up before he goes to the first tee. Somehow, very few of us would feel quite right about doing this in preparation for an afternoon round with several friends, for, although we may be anxious to play well, we do not like to make the impression that we are too anxious to win.

Even so, the preliminary warming up does not account for everything. Driving balls from a practice tee limbers up the muscles, but it does not furnish a test of the swing under conditions of actual play.

In the same way that Billy Burke describes, I am always very cautious in playing the first few shots, or the first few holes, of any round of golf. I think it is extremely important to feel one's way into the game, rather than to walk out on the first tee and "whale away" at the opening tee shot. I always like to know to what pitch my game is tuned before I begin to take any chances, either with my swing or in attempting difficult shots.

I have found that I am not alone in dreading the opening round of an important championship. Nearly all the players will tell you that the first round is certainly more difficult than the second, and is likely the most difficult of all except the last, where the intense strain of the finish comes in. In exactly the same way, I think you will also find that in each round the first few holes are the most difficult. One will rarely find a competitor who begins with any great expectation of setting the woods afire before he has thoroughly tested his game. He simply will not make any effort to begin picking up strokes until he has steadied himself and settled down with complete confidence to the job he has to do.

Swing Easy First Few Shots

My advice would always be to swing easily on the first few shots; to think more of placing the first tee shot down the fairway than of driving it a prodigious distance, and then to increase the power of the stroke gradually, putting just a little more steam into each drive until complete confidence has been achieved.

In the same way, I think it is always a good idea to play the first few iron shots with clubs which are able to obtain the necessary distance comfortably, always directing the shot toward the wide part of the green, safely away from trouble. I usually find that my best rounds in competition start easily and conservatively with a drive down the middle, an iron to the green and two putts.

Whenever the first four or five holes can be taken this way comfortably in par figures, then the rest of it seems to go along nicely. If, on the other hand, a too ambitious beginning causes the loss of several strokes at the start, it is sometimes impossible to get oneself in line and assume command of the game before the round or the match is over.

ON TINKERING WITH THE
GOLF SWING

I recall once receiving through the mail a pretty little leather-bound book which had on it in gold letters, "What I Know About Golf." When I opened it, I discovered that all the pages were blank—a handy little memorandum book. Since that time I have thought how nearly true was the message of that little book, and of how the game itself would impress that message upon us all if we stuck to it long enough.

There ought not to be anything so very mysterious about whacking a little ball down a fairway and finally rolling it into a fair-sized hole. To watch someone who really knows how convinces us that it isn't actually so difficult. But golf is the one game that I know which becomes more and more difficult the longer one plays it. A person may continue to improve his game from year to year, and each season may find him returning better scores, but as his skill increases and his understanding broadens, he will find that he is carrying a bigger load, that more severe demands are being made upon his concentration; in short, that he is having to work much harder than he ever did before. As his play has improved, his standards and expectations have moved out commensurately, and he is less tolerant with his mistakes. He soon finds that in order to play what he considers to be his "game," he has to watch himself far more closely than he did when his skill was less.

I think that the happiest moments for the golfer are those that he spends in study and experimentation. I should like to convince every player of the game, no matter to what stage he had progressed, that he will never arrive at any method or conception of the stroke to which he will be able to adhere rigidly throughout his golfing life. There are fundamentals which cannot be disregarded. To recognize these and to incorporate them in his swing will mean that his method will be basically sound. But from this point on, there will always be something to tinker with, new ideas to try, and old kinks to iron out.

> But golf is the one game that I know
> which becomes more and more difficult
> the longer one plays it.

I realize that I have advised sticking to one method or style after it has been developed along the right line. I still insist on this as the most practical course. There is no reason why any radical change should have to be made, but as the player progresses, he will find possibilities and problems in the game which in his less advanced state he had not dreamed of. These will be the things with which he will struggle, continually striving to make his performance more regular and efficient.

I doubt if anyone has ever been wholly satisfied with his golf; certainly if one has been so for the moment, the happy state has not endured for long. One who has had long experience, therefore, hesitates to lay down any rules to induce anyone to think that, beyond fundamentals, anything very definite can be prescribed. It is for the student to taste the joy of discovering for himself the "feel" of his club and of his muscles that leads to a fine shot. After he has passed the elemental stages, he will find that most of what he reads and hears from his pro will be merely reports from other experimenters, more experienced perhaps, but in other particulars like himself.

104

ON REQUIREMENTS OF
A GOOD BACKSWING

It is often urged that a person playing golf who worries about how to take the club back, how to start it down, and what to do at this stage and at that, ultimately loses sight of the only important thing he has to do—to hit the ball. We, who write about the game and attempt to teach it, are told often enough that we should give more attention to the contact stage and less to the details of the preparatory motions.

> The important points are the left arm,
> the left shoulder, the turn of the body,
> and the cock of the wrists.

It is true, of course, that it is not impossible to hit an occasional good shot even though all the teachings and practice of the experts in fundamentals are disregarded. But one who takes the long-range viewpoint cannot fail to appreciate that the basis of consistent and reliable performance must be good form. There are certain actions which must take place during the act of hitting, if the ball is to be struck with accuracy and power. A haphazard, uninformed player, once in a while may find himself in position to complete these actions, but he cannot hope to compete successfully with the man whose sound swing carries him, time after time, into this position.

A Correct Sequence

The downward or hitting stroke is intended to culminate in a well-timed, powerful contact between clubhead and ball. There is no way to argue that the successful accomplishment of this purpose is not the most important part of the stroke.

But the backswing has for its purpose the establishment of a perfectly balanced, powerful position at the top of the swing from which the correct actions of the downstroke can flow rhythmically without the need for interference or correction.

In the end, on the basis of consistent reproduction of the successful faction, the preparatory movements become just as important as the actual hitting—the entire swing, a sequence of correct positions, following naturally and comfortably one after the other.

I think it is easier to understand the requirements of a good backswing if one looks first at the things that it is designed to accomplish. The important points are the left arm, the left shoulder, the turn of the body, and the cock of the wrists. The fact that the hands are higher than the head and the shaft of the club is pointing to the right of the objective is also worth noting.

Straight Left Arm Governs Arc

The straightness of the left arm accomplishes, or at least makes possible, a number of desirable things. First and most important, its full extension, maintained throughout from the start of the backswing until impact, causes the arc of the swing to be very wide, and this increases its potential power. Likewise, since the distance from the left shoulder to the left hand is constant as long as the left elbow remains unbent, the straight left, in the only possible way, locates the arm of the swing where it can be retraced times without number. It is plain, too, that the left arm owes its opportunity to remain straight to the fact that the right arm is relaxed and is a willing follower.

This suggests what I deem to be the proper procedure; namely, that the club should be swung back mainly by pushing it with the left arm. This tends to avoid the common mistake of picking the club up abruptly with the right hand, and likewise materially encourages a free turn of the hips and shoulders.

It will be seen also that the shoulders have not turned in the same plane. The left shoulder is now several inches lower than the right, whereas it was itself higher when addressing the ball. The turn has been very full, but dipping the left shoulder has permitted the location of the head and the axis of the shoulders to remain unchanged.

ON MAKING
EACH SHOT COUNT

In every sport, and, I suppose, in almost every other line of endeavor, it is hard to separate and recognize the qualities which distinguish the great from the near-great—the men who succeed from those who just can't quite make it. In golf, this little difference, as telling as it is, is yet so small that it is difficult to see how it can be a definite advantage.

> And we ought to see also that in a medal round, to hole a long putt for a six is just as good as if it were for a three. It is every shot that counts.

I remember reading in an English newspaper, after I had won the British open at St. Andrews, an editorial that made a point of how slight a margin of superiority was shown by the winner of a tournament over the rest of the field. In this particular championship, I had won by the greatest margin I had ever had yet, as the editorial pointed out. My advantage of six strokes, however big it may have looked, when reduced to percentage was only 2.105 per cent, or one and one-half strokes in each round in which an average of a little less than seventy-two strokes was used.

I suppose it is consideration of a slender margin such as

this that leads J. H. Taylor to say that the difference between a winner and the near-winner is the ability on the part of the successful contestant to be ever on the lookout against himself. Never too certain of what the result may be, he never plays a shot carelessly or with overconfidence.

Average Counts

In competition, I have never regarded seriously the tendency of some people to endow certain golfers with superhuman powers. Because, on occasions, certain players have staged spectacular finishes to retrieve a victory by a last-minute rally. I have heard it said of them that they are able to pull off whatever is necessary to win. Such an idea is absurd, for if these men were capable of playing golf as they willed, they would never place themselves in a position where they had to beat par to win. And when I hear someone criticized for "cracking" at the finish, I always think of the query that Grantland Rice propounded at Scioto—whether it was better to blow up in the third round or the fourth. Every player has his bad patches in any 72-hole journey. It is mainly a question of who averages up the best over the entire route, and that, I think, is the feature that the winner remembers and the field forgets.

Each Shot Important

When we begin to think in terms of the English editorial I have referred to, we must see the importance of each stroke, whether it be drive, approach, or putt. And we ought to see also that in a medal round, to hole a long putt for a six is just as good as if it were for a three. It is every shot that counts.

In defining the difference between the great and the near-great, J.H. Taylor pointed out a lesson for every golfer. He was

not merely explaining why some fine golfers win championships and others equally fine do not. He was telling you why
you missed that easy pitch to the fourth green yesterday and
why, after you had missed your second shot to the eighth, you
took a seven instead of the five you should have had, if you
had played sensibly. All of us, from duffers to champions,
would do better if we would play each shot as a thing to itself.

THE PRACTICE SWING
IN PRACTICE

There is not one golfer in the world who has not, at some time, thought how fine it would be if he could swing at the ball as freely and as smoothly as he swings at a dandelion or a piece of paper lying on the grass. Some, indeed, do not even then have the graceful and effective appearance to others that they conceive themselves to have, but there is no denying, except in the case of experts, that the practice swing is, almost always, by far the better of the two. And the player himself senses and admits this difference, often recognizes the reason, yet fails to understand that there is a sensible way to gradually overcome it.

Most people accept it as one of those things which must be suffered. The necessity for the existence of this difference is lamented, accepted, and we pass on. The entire business is attributed to a mental condition, a sense of responsibility, anxiety, fear, or whatnot, which sets up a tension that cannot be overcome.

This much is true, but it so happens that it is only a part of the story. The difference in the state of mind of the player, when taking a practice swing and when playing an actual stroke, is easily understood and its effect appreciated, but what is neither understood nor appreciated is that the elimination or omission of some of the frills of the actual stroke which are not present in the practice swing may work a com-

plete change. The expert is not afraid of the ball because he
has learned to have confidence in his ability to hit it.

Avoid Tenseness

Watch a moderately good average golfer take a practice
swing preparatory to making a shot. He swings the club easily,
rhythmically to and fro; there is a decent balance throughout
and a commendable relaxation. The stance is always conservative and comfortable—one into which he has stepped naturally, without any fuss or bother. Now, watch him as he steps
up to the ball. He first sets his feet wide apart—at least farther
apart than they were before. That is to assure good balance
and a firm footing.

> The general criticisms which are to be
> made of the average player's posture at
> address are that his feet are too far
> apart, his body is bent too much, and
> his arms are extended too far.

Then he begins to waggle, and the more he waggles, the
more he bends over the ball, and the more tense he becomes.
Instead of sensing the proper position or of falling naturally
into a comfortable one, he attempts to set himself before the
ball with perfect accuracy, attempting to see that everything is
placed just so.

Things to Avoid

I have no quarrel with anyone for taking pains with a shot
and for making certain that he is ready to play before he starts

the swing. But most golfers lose sight of the fact that in the first position it is ease and comfort that are to be found, and that a strained or unnatural posture was never intended by anyone.

The general criticisms which are to be made of the average player's posture at address are that his feet are too far apart, his body is bent too much, and his arms are extended too far. These are the commonest faults, and every one of them is unnatural. The natural way to stand is with the feet separated but not set wide apart; the natural bend of the body is very slight, with the weight more back on the heels and never entirely on the toes, and the natural position of the arms is hanging almost straight down, close in to the body.

It is very rare that tension is observed in a practice swing, and this is so because the player, not feeling the necessity of being entirely correct, comes closer to assuming a natural posture. Let him take this naturalness into the actual shot; let him simplify his preliminary motions as much as possible, and let him start the ball on its way without hurry, yet without setting himself on point before it, like a fine dog on a covey of quail. In this way, he can go a long way on the physical side toward overcoming the understandable mental processes which must arise when the responsibility of hitting the ball confronts him. Mental tension; that is, keenness, never does any harm when it is accompanied by physical relaxation.

On Good Fortune and Sudden Disaster in Championships

It is certainly an old and familiar saying that any one man has to be lucky to win an open championship, and this is true even of one who may be entitled to be considered the best man in the field. This may be a bit hard for some people to appreciate—why it is not possible to pick even three or four men, and say that the winner will be one of the three or four.

> But I think the most dreadful things are the sudden disasters that can befall one in an open championship.

Of course, one of the chief reasons is the almost unbelievable inconsistency of form. I have seen any number of instances where a man would be playing perfect golf right up to the day before a tournament, and then become suddenly helpless when the competition had gotten under way. And on the other hand, I have seen reversals just as startling in the other direction. The case of Gene Sarazen at Winged Foot in 1929 is a fine example. I played with Gene in a four-ball the day before the open began, and in all the time I have known him, I have never seen him play so badly, and that at the time embraced a stretch of over ten years. Every shot was going wrong. His score was in the middle eighties somewhere, and I

Gene Sarazen and Bob Jones

had not the slightest idea that he would be able to pull his game sufficiently together to even make a showing. Yet Gene led off, right off the bat, with two fine rounds, and was in the fight right up to the last nine holes. He didn't win, but he did just what a winner has to be lucky enough to do—find his game at the right time.

But I think the most dreadful things are the sudden disasters that can befall one in an open championship. It is impossible to explain or account for them. They simply happen, and that's all there is to it. You will be going alone serenely enough, with no particular worries on your mind, when bang!—there goes a seven or an eight, and you can't figure out how it happened.

> I took a seven when, as Bernard Darwin said, "An old lady with a broom handle could have holed out in five."

In the last round of this same championship at Winged Foot that I mentioned a few seconds before, I was moving along quite satisfactorily through the seventh hole. I had started off in the lead, and was hitting the ball just as well as I could want to, a stroke better than par through number seven, and reports kept coming back to me that everybody else was blowing up. I needed two fours to be out in 35, and there would be nothing more to the championship. At the eighth hole I cut my second shot only a little bit into a bunker at the right of the green. Still that was all right—I had strokes to spare. But I blasted from that bunker across the green into one on the other side, and from there back to the one I had been in first, and before I knew it I had rolled up a 7. Instead of being calm and confident as I had been up to that point, I was now rattled and afraid of my shadow. I picked up another 7 coming home, and only managed to tie by the grace of good fortune and my early lead. I might just as well have played my-self out of the tournament on that eighth hole.

In the same situation at Olympia Fields, when everything seemed settled after I had passed the difficult part of the course in the first five holes, I suddenly lost all idea of how to hit a golf ball, and in the next five holes I lost seven strokes to par. And then again at Hoylake last year, after two good shots to the eighth against a stiff breeze, where my ball lay only fif-teen yards off the putting surface. I took a seven when, as Bernard Darwin said, "An old lady with a broom handle could have holed out in five."

ON THE IMPORTANCE OF
THE CLUB FACE AT IMPACT

After all, when we consider the limitless number of different situations that come up in even a week of golf, and the vastly different characteristics, mental and physical, of the individuals who play the game, it is not hard to see why it is so difficult to prescribe Thus and So to be a general rule. The professional teacher giving private lessons has some chance. If he knows his job, he will be able to teach and correct, starting at some point that he will select as the foundation point of his pupil's swing. But because his problem is balancing every motion in proper relation to all the others, there is no possibility of a general or shotgun prescription being able to take his place. The best that anyone in my position can hope to do is to assist somewhat in giving the player or pupil the proper conception of what he should attempt to do, leaving the business of developing the swing to his personal instructor.

Within a maze of straight left arms, lateral hip-shots, slow backswings and cocked left wrists, sometimes I think there is danger of losing sight of the end to which we are driving. These things are details. We might even say they are niceties which we look for in the more highly developed swings of the experts. But I think the beginner would serve himself best if he would forget these refinements during the early stages of his golfing growth. By all means let him first understand what it is that produces the well-directed shot for which he is striving so hard.

The things I am going to say are almost absurdly simple,

but I believe they are things too seldom remembered. The first one is that a straight shot is most efficiently produced when the club face at the instant of impact is square or at right angles to the line of flight, and when the direction of its motion is along this line. Everyone knows that. It just can't be any other way. Any other alignment of the face or direction of motion must impart some side spin to the ball. Yet don't we forget that this, instead of a straight left arm, is the end we are striving for? The straight left has been found to be of help in reaching the ideal, but is not itself that ideal.

Within a maze of straight left arms, lateral hip-shots, slow backswings and cocked left wrists, sometimes I think there is danger of losing sight of the end to which we are driving.

There certainly are more ways than one of playing good golf, let us say, of bringing the club face into the correct hitting position at the right time. You need only to watch an open championship to be convinced of this. Since this is so, would not the beginner, before he concerns himself too much with refinements of style, be better off if he would merely keep before him a clear picture of what he was trying to do with the club? Would he not be able to develop himself more rapidly if he would remember that the errors in his shots are the results of errors in his club at impact, either in alignment or in direction of motion? Remembering this seems to me to give him a better chance of trial and error, to use what he may be told, along with his own experience.

ON POWER IN THE DRIVE

There are more than a few golfers in this land who wonder why and how it is, that even when they connect sweetly with a drive, it never goes as far as an ordinary shot by a youth of much less physical power. Most of all, it puzzles the brawny athletes who still possess brawn and muscle far exceeding that of any first-class golfer in the game today. They cannot understand how a little 120-pound kid can stand up all day long and wallop out drives far beyond the very best efforts they could produce in a year.

Physical strength does count for something in golf. It would be foolish to say that it did not, for although we may talk all we please about rhythm, timing, and whatnot, still the fact remains that the man who hits the ball the hardest will achieve the longest drive. Rhythm, timing, and the other essentials of form merely determine which player can deliver the hardest blow.

Good Timing Aids

Long driving, up to a certain point, may be explained by good timing. By this I mean that the increased length obtained by the whole rank of first-class players over that obtained by the second-class can be largely attributed to better timing. The dub suffers because he rarely expends his power where it will do the most good. But within the group of players which we refer to as the first class, there are a few who are able to drive a good bit farther than any of their fellows. This increase, I think, is not explainable on the basis of timing, for all of the better players are good in this respect; these extra yards obtainable by the few are traceable to form, and not timing.

Long Drivers Have Fast Pivot

Every now and then even the average golfer will meet the ball exactly right—as far as timing and feel are concerned. When he does so, he reaches the ultimate for him. Yet a more proficient player of much less physical strength has no difficulty in passing, by many yards, his longest drive. The things which make this possible are to be found in the swing—the increased body turn, the hands high at the top of the backswing, the length and greater fullness of the arc.

The longest hitters in the world today are Charles Lacy, Charlie Hall, Cyril Tolley, Bill Stout, and a Frenchman, Marcel Dallmagne. A noticeable feature of the style of each is a fast pivot or hip turn, as the club approaches the ball coming down. They make the best use of the most powerful muscles of the body, those of the back and trunk, and hitting so they gain over the rest of the field those few extra yards that make them stand out.

The average golfer uses his hips and body very little. He takes the club back with his arms mainly, and he hits without making any great effort with the muscles of his back. The player who is a little better, but still not expert, turns more; he may even turn back quite nicely, but an observer will note that his turn into the ball is retarded—he may even stop his pivot before he hits the ball. The expert next employs a full turn and continues his turn forward uninterrupted through the

122

hitting area, and the very long driver whips his hips around like a flash.

A Mighty Atom

I have never seen a more impressive demonstration of what form will accomplish than was given by little Norman Maxwell in a game in Atlanta back about 1915. Norman was then a very small chap—he could not have weighed over 120 pounds—with tiny wrists and arms. He and Ned Beall came down to Atlanta from Pinehurst to play a return match against Perry Adair and me, after they had given us an artistic lacing at the North Carolina resort. I have not seen Maxwell play since that day, but I remember his swing as perfectly as if I had seen it yesterday. He possessed the two characteristics of the long hitter—a wide sweeping arc with the hands well above the head at the top of the swing, and the fast body turn into the ball. In thirty-six holes of that match, on soggy turf, he hit the ball distances that had never been seen in Atlanta before, and were not seen again until Cyril Tolley arrived in 1924 with the real big guns.

THE OLD COURSE

A fter reading of the wonderfully low scores returned at St. Andrews in the qualifying and early rounds of the British open championship, I could see that critics of the old course would most likely renew their claim that the course was too easy, and that even some of those who love it might begin to ask themselves questions. It was not bad, of course, for Nolan to go around in 67, nor for Hagen to follow the next day with a 68. These two scores might have been, and unquestionably were, the results of magnificent golf. But what would start the talk was the number of scores in the low 70s which followed the leader on each day. Scores like these do not turn up in such profusion even in a great field like this, on a really difficult golf course.

No one loves that old course any more than I do, yet I do not mind admitting that under certain conditions it can be comparatively simple. It was relatively easy when we played the open there in 1927.

Variety is a Key

But it seems to me that the very fact that the course can be easy when it can likewise be very difficult is a virtue rather than a fault, because it is an indication of the variety that can be found there. The only course that will remain difficult under all conditions will be one that is designed and kept for golf of a stereotyped, monotonous character, and this makes a most uninteresting proposition.

Unfortunately, one finds too many courses of this nature in America. Our tendencies over here have been to lengthen the holes, and to pull the bunkers closer in to the greens, in order to provide an examination in mechanical skill. The interest and delight in playing a fascinating game have been all but submerged because of an insane desire to keep record scores up, and to provide an exacting test which will make the big shot sweat and the average golfer tear his hair.

Any course should have a fair sprinkling of long holes to afford opportunities for playing shots with all the clubs in the bag. But on some courses, the playing of these shots and these holes becomes a task rather than a privilege. Too often, we have overlooked the fact that a hole of three hundred and twenty to fifty yards can be a perfect delight to play, even with a green considerably larger than a postage stamp.

> The only course that will remain difficult under all conditions will be one that is designed and kept for golf of a stereotyped, monotonous character, and this makes a most uninteresting proposition.

In this country, we delight to pitch, pitch, pitch, because it is easier than executing a delicate run-up or pitch-and-run. And, insisting upon pitching, we also insist that our greens be kept so that we can pitch, whether skillfully or not, on all occasions. The result has been that we expect to bang every shot to the green, and the only variety of our play comes from conditions of wind or fairway, which determine whether the pitch shall be long or short.

The first nine at St. Andrews is relatively short on total length. On the first day of the recent championship, the wind was behind all the way out. This is a condition frequently met, and when the greens are firm it makes necessary quite a lot of local knowledge and maneuvering to play into positions from which the ball can be stopped near the hole. It is then the most fascinating kind of golf. But, according to Hagen, the greens had been wetted, and it was possible to pitch, which created precisely the conditions we met in 1927. Pitching to every green, of course, all subtlety disappears, and the play becomes much simpler. But these are watered only when unusual weather creates a dire necessity, or when Pluvius, the Latin god of rain, takes a hand. The conditions are thus as variable as the weather, which is plenty.

VARDON'S LESSON

It has not been difficult to make a majority of golfers understand that the controlled shot in golf—the shot intended to
carry some amount of backspin—should be accomplished by
a stroke which brings the clubhead against the ball on the descending arc. Almost everyone recognizes the divot-taking
stroke which the expert employs with his iron clubs, so it is
common knowledge that with these implements it is proper to
"hit down." But in this respect, as in many others, the degree
to which the thing is done is of great importance. It is impossible to think of a golfing virtue which cannot be exaggerated
or emphasized into a fault.

> I was moving yards of turf at each
> stroke, and giving my wrists an awful
> pounding, but I continued to hook,
> smother, and top shots indiscriminately.

When I was a small boy, twelve or thirteen years old, I
think, I remember being much inspired by an article over
Harry Vardon's signature describing the correct method of
executing a "push shot." Prior to that time, I had heard a lot
about the push shot and had read numerous mentions of it,
but I had never seen one played—that is, as I had conceived

it, although I had watched some pretty fair players, among them old Harry himself. I even had asked Stewart Maiden about it, but Stewart was never fond of frills, and he always put me off with some joking response.

Giving It a Try

So when I ran across this article of Vardon's, I decided to give the push shot a try. I read the piece through, then reread it; then I boarded an electric car and took the article with me to a practice tee at East Lake. Stewart was giving a lesson on the adjoining tee, but I dared not interrupt him, and soon I became so occupied with my article and the push shot that I forgot anyone was near. The idea, of course, was to deliver a sharply descending blow which would produce a low-flying shot which would bring up relatively quickly after striking the ground. The low trajectory was all I was ever able to get. I was moving yards of turf at each stroke, and giving my wrists an awful pounding, but I continued to hook, smother, and top shots indiscriminately.

> As I looked back he chuckled again.
> "What are ye trying to do, Robin?
> Move the golf course?"

But I was still taking myself seriously when I heard a soft chuckle behind. I turned at the sound and found Stewart perched on a bench, with cap cocked up on the back of his head and having the time of his life watching me. As I looked back he chuckled again. "What are ye trying to do, Robin? Move the golf course?" was all he ever said, but I have never troubled about the push shot since.

Too Much Medicine

I confess that to this day I do not know if the push shot ever existed as a shot distinct from the ordinary low-flying iron shot that we employ today to meet certain conditions. I am certain of one thing, which is that Harry Vardon never intended that the shot should be played as I attempted to play it. I am familiar with the low iron shot, played somewhat less than full into a head wind. This shot is "hit down" slightly more than the perfectly straightforward type, but ever so slightly more.

I believe this was Vardon's meaning, which I decided to go one better, like the patient who thought that if a tablespoonful of medicine would do him good, the whole bottle taken immediately would effect a cure. At any rate, for better or for worse, Stewart Maiden laughed me out of any further concern with the push shot. After that little experience, whenever anyone mentioned it to me, I would change the subject as rapidly as possible.

SWING THE CLUBHEAD

Two of golf's most eminent instructors, Macdonald Smith and Ernest Jones, build all their teaching around the one conception, "Swing the clubhead with a decided stress on the swing." There are other details to be thought of, of course, in developing anything like a sound swing, but in the end it will be found that this is the prime necessity. Those who are able to sense what it means to "swing the clubhead" will find that they can thus cover up a multitude of sins, and those who sense it not will find that no degree of painstaking perfection will quite take its place.

> The club must be swung back far
> enough so that there will be no need for
> hurry or quickened effort coming down.

In order to make easier the discovery of this sense of swinging, the club must be swung back far enough so that there will be no need for hurry or quickened effort coming down. This is the one point that I have tried to stress more than anything else—the necessity for an ample back swing—and it is one of the first things that has to be done in order to "swing the clubhead." The man who allows himself only a short back swing can never be a swinger, because his abbreviated length does not give him space for an easy acceleration to get him "up to speed," as they say in the movies, by the time the club reaches the ball.

A Crucial Point

Rhythm and timing are the two things that we all must have, yet no one knows how to teach either. The nearest approach to an accurate description of what they are is found in the expression of this conception of swinging. The man who hits *at* the ball rather than *through* it has no sense of rhythm. Similarly, the man who, after a short back swing, attempts to make up for lost space by convulsive effort initiating the downstroke, has no sense of rhythm.

The only one who has a chance to achieve a rhythmic, well-timed stroke is the man who, in spite of all else, yet "swings his clubhead." And the crucial area is when the swing changes direction at the top. If the backswing can be made to flow back leisurely and to an ample length, whence the start downward can be made without the feeling that there may not be enough time left, there is a good chance of success. But a hurried backswing induces a hurried start downward, and a short backswing makes some sort of rescue measures imperative. A good golfer will not like to be guilty of either.

Clubhead Must Be Felt

Two of the important points in the swinging machinery are the wrists and hips. If the former do not flex easily or if the latter do not turn readily, a true swing cannot be accomplished. Stiff or wooden wrists shorten the backswing and otherwise destroy the "feel" of the clubhead. Without the supple connection of relaxed and active wrist joints and a delicate sensitive grip, the golf club which has been so carefully weighted and balanced might just as well be a broom handle with nothing on the end. The clubhead cannot be swung unless it can be felt to be on the end of the shaft.

So swing, swing, swing, if you want to play better golf! Fight down any tautness wherever it may make its appearance. Strive for relaxed muscles throughout, and encourage a feeling of laziness in the backswing and the start downward. Go back far enough, trust your swing, and then—swing the clubhead through.

Don't Pounce

Our notion of the golf swing has changed much in the past thirty years. Principally by the aid of improved photography, both motion picture and the still ultraspeed exposure, we have been able to learn much—to obtain a demonstration of things we could only guess at before, and to disprove certain ideas we could arrive at only by feel. But the analytical exposition of the golf swing, when it is slowed down or stopped for examination, reveals nothing of rhythm or timing. For these, we must go to an actual observation of the swing itself, or to the player himself to tell us the beat he swings in.

I have chanced upon a thing written by Harold Hilton in 1903 which so closely parallels what I myself have written and said so many times that the similarity was startling. A comparison of this and present-day utterances shows that the rhythm of the well-timed swing has not been altered much through the change of implements and balls.

Mr. Hilton wrote of S. Mure Ferguson, one of the long drivers of that era:

"On the upward swing Mr. Ferguson always appears to take the club up in a most leisurely and deliberate fashion and maintains this leisurely method at the beginning of the downward swing; in fact he always appears to be swinging slowly and well within himself, and this probably accounts for the fine free action of the body when following through; but by the length of ball he drives it is manifest that the clubhead must be traveling fast when it reaches the ball."

Of this passage, the most important part is to be found in the statement that Mr. Ferguson "maintains this leisurely method at the beginning of the downward swing." We hear "slow back" on every side, but "slow back" is not enough. There are numbers of players who are able to restrain their impulses to this extent, but who, once back, literally pounce upon the ball with uncontrolled fury. It is the leisurely start downward that provides for a gradual increase of speed without disturbing the balance and timing of the swing.

Henry Cotton in a recent article relates how Tommy Armour started badly in the latest British open because his tee shots were ill-timed, and hence decidedly wild; and when they were straight, they were very short. According to Cotton, Armour forced himself to swing more and more slowly until he felt that he would never complete the stroke at all. Finally, in this way, he worked himself back into his proper rhythm and had no more trouble.

I am not a believer in very heavy clubs. But there is no doubt that a heavier club tends to slow up one's swing to an extent which is sometimes very helpful. It is certainly true that the same club does not feel the same every day and under all conditions. Sometimes it is worthwhile to try a club with a little additional weight if the swing is found to be a bit too fast.

But in any event, strive for rhythm. Let the backswing and the start downward be leisurely. I like this better than "slow," because a swing might be too painfully slow. And always remember that there is plenty of space and time to gather speed between the top of the swing and the ball.

ON COORDINATING THE LEFT AND RIGHT HANDS

Both hands are essential to making a stroke, and contribute a material part to developing the speed of the clubhead. The right hand functions chiefly in increasing the speed as the clubhead nears the ball. It can, and will, jam things up if it gets into the stroke too early, and it often does by getting in too vigorously when it does enter. The right hand is a difficult factor to control in a golf swing, because it is working more or less "on the loose," with no anchor to hold it down. Those persons who say that the right packs more power than the left may be correct, but the trouble is that the average person can't help using his right, and needs to be told constantly to use his left more.

That's what the first player mentioned in the previous paragraph had in mind when he spoke of keeping his right hand out of the swing. And that, too, is what the professional, who had been instructing the other, had in mind in the suggestion to change the position of the left hand on the club, although he did not tell the pupil so in so many words.

It is not hard to prove that the besetting sin with the vast army of golfers is a failure to hit through with the left arm and hand, as well as by a tendency to permit the right to overpower the left. The inclination is to practically stop the forward sweep of the left arm as the effort is made to snap the head through with the right. And the main trouble is that the

135

right snaps too soon, overpowering the left, resulting in the hook which one of the men referred to above was getting.

Left Arm Action

The action by the left arm in swinging the club through obviously enough is a backhanded one, and to make it as effective as possible it should be entirely backhanded; that is, the left hand should be so placed that a direct straight pull is possible by the outside muscles of the left arm from the shoulder to the elbow.

Possibly the idea I am trying to convey will be made somewhat clearer by the following: Stretch the left arm straight out in front of the shoulder, with the palm facing straight down to the ground. Now drop the arm from that position straight down to the side. The wrist and forearm are now in the position which yields the fullest power for striking a backhand blow with the arm. This in effect was what the instructor was doing with the player above, in giving him a new position on the club for that left hand.

In making the backswing, avoid turning the wrist of the left arm away from that position any more than is necessary. If you maintain that position with the wrist at the top of the swing, you will have the left arm set to do its most effective work in swinging the clubhead through. See that the left arm swings straight on out after the ball, as far as it will reach. Don't bother about the turning over of the right wrist. This will take care of itself. Anyway, slow-motion action pictures have shown clearly that this turning over doesn't take place until well after the ball has been hit. Only when it takes place too soon does it have any effect on the shot, and that effect is always bad.

On a Smooth, Simple Repeating Swing

The average golfer who takes his golf even a little seriously certainly might be pardoned for wondering just what the experts mean when they point out so and so as the possessor of "a fine, sound style." Soundness is recognized by all as a most desirable attribute of a golf swing, but I am afraid that merely to point out that such a one possesses that virtue affords little help to the fellow who would give his right arm to be sound, too. Too many times we, who are interested in offering what help we can to those who want it, are too willing to pass over, with such an unenlightening phrase, the very things in which the struggling beginner is most interested. There ought at least to be understood what kind of swing we mean, and what it is that makes a method sound.

Simplicity Keynote

Obviously, the sound swing is not a definite reality. We all recognize that no two players swing a club in exactly the same manner, yet certainly more than one deserves to be regarded as a sound swinger. The trained observer and student of the game over a long period of close observance and intimate contact with successful players in time fixes upon several actions and postures which are common to all. He learns to separate the mannerisms of the individual from the basic elements of his swing, and gradually he builds up a conception of a correct set of motions which he regards as essential in playing the game expertly. When he says that a certain swing is sound, he means that regardless of the variations peculiar to the individual, the method still embraces and accounts for all of the correct actions and postures, or enough of them to assure a high degree of success.

The first requisite of a truly sound swing is simplicity. In this respect I think that Horton Smith and Miss Joyce Wethered excel all golfers. In the case of each, the matter of hitting the ball has been reduced to two motions, taking the club back with one, and bringing it down with the other. I have found many to agree with me that Miss Wethered's swing is the most perfect in the world, but I think it is safe to say that Horton Smith's backswing is the simplest in the world. Either of these two makes an ideal model to be imitated by everyone, for in these two methods it is possible to see all of the fundamentals, without the confusing effect of a great many mannerisms.

We all recognize that no two players swing a club in exactly the same manner, yet certainly more than one deserves to be regarded as a sound swinger.

It will be found also that the sound swing is a very graceful one. That does not mean that any graceful motion is necessarily sound, but one cannot execute the various motions nor assume successively the correct postures in rhythmic style without effecting a very pleasing look. The sound swing flows from beginning to end, but it flows powerfully and is graceful because it is correct, rather than because it is made so. I know that all of us have seen many swings which were pretty enough, but were so only because the player sacrificed power for appearance.

Reproducing Same Swing

There is at least one thing more that the sound swinger must possess, and that is the ability to reproduce, time and again, the same old performance. In the end, this virtue includes at least the first I have named, for in order to be capable of endless reproduction, the swing must be simple.

The one point where it is of the utmost importance that the player is in the correct position occurs at the time when he strikes the ball. A good many players, by an extraordinary action of one kind or another, manage to right themselves at impact a great part of the time. These are the fellows who play excellent golf almost all of the time, yet not quite consistently enough, under a big strain, to win important championships. It takes a sound swing, fundamentally correct, to stand the gaff of competition.

ON THE GREATEST MATCHES
EVER PLAYED

From time to time, I suppose I have been asked on half a hundred occasions what was, in my opinion, the greatest golf match ever played. In answering a question of this kind, I do not like to go beyond my personal observation, and in placing myself on record, I do not believe I can afford to take in quite this much territory. I have never yet been present at a P.G.A. championship, where, I am sure, a great many fine matches have been played. But I have seen most of the best encounters in the American amateur championship since 1916, and in three British amateurs since 1921.

> But in all the long history of the game,
> I think there has never been a recovery
> as brilliantly accomplished against so
> uncompromising an opponent.

A few of the outstanding matches which I could name without hesitation were as follows: The match between Chick Evans and Francis Ouimet at Oakmont in 1919; the match between Travers and Hagen at Garden City in the P.G.A. war relief matches of 1917; the match between Marston and Sweetser in the American amateur championship of 1923 at Flossmoor; the match between Von Elm and Hezlet in the

Walker cup bout at St. Andrews in 1926; and the match between Don Moe and Bill Stout at Sandwich in the international match in 1930.

That Herreshoff-Hilton Match

Of course, the old-timers probably will say that no list of outstanding matches is complete without mention of the historic Herreshoff-Hilton match at Apawamis in 1911, when the great little Englishman won our amateur championship on the thirty-seventh green. But that was considerably before my time. In later years, I suppose that the Hagen-Sarazen affair at Pelham in the finals of the P.G.A. championship of 1923 should also come in. But my testimony with respect to that is likewise incompetent.

To pick out one match from the list enumerated above is a pretty tough assignment, but I think that for pure, unadulterated sensation the Moe-Stout match puts it pretty well over the others. Each of the other four tussles was a dogfight from start to finish, with both contestants at one another's throat throughout the match, with never a commanding advantage on either side. But in all the long history of the game, I think there has never been a recovery as brilliantly accomplished against so uncompromising an opponent.

A Great Comeback

In many respects, a comparison between this match and the famous Von Elm-MacKenzie encounter at Merion in 1924 would show a close parallel, except for two important facts. First, MacKenzie did not win, although his brilliant rally carried the match to the thirty-seventh green after he had been 8 down with 14 holes to play; and, second, Von Elm in losing his big lead made a few more mistakes than did Bill Stout against Moe.

That Moe-Stout match is more or less recent history, and its details are so well recalled that it is not necessary to recount them. But a brief resume will serve to show what a tremendous thing it was. Young Don, playing in his first competition abroad, found the long-driving Englishman in one of his most devastating moods, and in the morning round he bumped squarely into a fine 71 by Stout. That left Don 4 down at lunchtime, and in the afternoon Stout opened up 3-3-3, which made the margin 7 holes with fifteen to play, and it looked as if the kid would be overwhelmed. But beginning with the fourth hole, Don shot the works. When I saw him hole a putt of six feet for a birdie 3 at the ninth green, after a grand pitch, it was his fifth 3 in six holes, and he continued in this vein until, when they stood on the thirty-sixth tee, the match was square, and then came the finish, which was entirely worthy of this marvelous effort. I wondered what poor Bill Stout must have thought, when, after all that had happened, he watched Don fire a long iron second from a hanging tie up stone dead against the pin.

It must be remembered that throughout this afternoon round, Stout himself was playing fine golf, and not giving away a thing. Moe's play during the afternoon round was most aptly characterized in an expostulation which Stout himself told me was made to him by one of his friends. After Don had won back five holes, Stout said, he was walking down the fairway, wondering what it was all about, when his friend touched him on the arm and said, "My word, Bill—this is not golf; it's visitation from God!"

143

Afterword

Even though today's golfers are bigger, stronger, and perhaps smarter than yesterday, they still don't know it all. It takes a genius with the secrets of the game to unlock the treasure chest of knowledge if you really want to understand what's going on. Bobby Jones knew the secrets of the game. And he wasn't bashful about sharing them with others. In articles for Jack Wheeler's Bell Syndicate, Jones wrote twice weekly columns in the 1920s about the secrets he used to conquer his opponents, Old Man Par, and himself on the links. As you have just seen, these secrets are not tarnished by the passage of time. Instead, they have been tested and found to be sound by those who followed Jones. Never mind that it required a superior intellect to conceive the proper physics of the golf swing, test it in the crucible of competition, and then express the concept of proper feel in words which can be read, understood, and translated by the common man into action in his Saturday gangsome. Jones could do this like no other champion in the history of the game. He could anticipate the difficulties, overcome them in practice, and describe the formula used by him to unlock the mystery. Jones believed that golf and golf courses are not unlike whimsical ladies. They must be studied to be understood and understood to be studied. The more you study, the more you understand, and the more you understand, the more you study. But knowledge is not enough. As you just discovered in these pages, some mysteries are only unlocked for us by pioneers— such as these secrets of the master.

—Sidney L. Matthew